HITLER'S
NAVAL
BASES

HITLER'S NAVAL BASES

KRIEGSMARINE BASES DURING THE SECOND WORLD WAR

JAK P. MALLMANN SHOWELL

FONTHILL

The sights of a small-calibre AA gun.

Fonthill Media Limited
Fonthill Media LLC
www.fonthill.media
books@fonthill.media

First published 2013
Reprinted 2020

British Library Cataloguing in Publication Data:
A catalogue record for this book is available from the British Library

ISBN 978-1-78155-198-1

Typeset in 9.5pt on 13pt Sabon
Printed and bound in England

Connect with us
 facebook.com/fonthillmedia   twitter.com/fonthillmedia

Contents

Introduction 7

1. German Naval Bases 9

2. Different Types of German Naval Bases 16

3. The Main Naval Bases in Germany 32

4. Major Bases that Never Were 61

5. Clandestine Centres 68

6. Lorient – The First and the Last 72
  Biscay Base in France

7. Joining the Naval Command Centre 88
  in Boulogne

8. Problems with Southern Europe 97

9. Far-Away Bases 105

10. Naval Artillery and Naval Infantry 120

11. Naval Fire Fighters 171

12. Sentries and Guards 181

13. Air Raid Shelters   185

14. Rules for Living in Naval Barracks   193

15. German Naval Bases   203

16. The Major Ship Building Yards of   241
                the Third Reich

   Glossary   243

   Bibliography   250

   Index   252

An armoured emergency door in the side of the flak tower at Wilhelmsburg (Hamburg).

Introduction

Much of the material for this book has come from Deutsches U-Boot-Museum in Cuxhaven-Altenbruch (www.dubm.de) and I am most grateful to its founder and director, Horst Bredow, for guiding me through his marvellous archive. During the research I made extensive use of the Werner Krauss collection and am delighted that this includes such helpful books. The Walter Schöppe Collection at the U-boat Museum also needs a special mention for having yielded some fascinating material. The individual sources used in this book have been acknowledged in the main text.

I should like to thank Kpt.z.S. a.D. Peter Monte for his interesting conducted tour of the naval relics in Cuxhaven, and I should also like to thank the following for helping with information and photographs: Graham George (for information about the Ashley Bombing Range in the New Forest), Hans-Jürgen Jürgens (for his fantastic book about the Frisian Islands), Arianne Krause, Wolfram Kroschel, Gregor Ulsamer (for his excellent book about coastal communications) and I must apologise if I have forgotten anyone.

Unless otherwise marked, photographs come from Deutsches U-Boot-Museum or from the author's collection.

The writing of this book started innocuously enough, but it wasn't long before the research yielded so much that one was more than overwhelmed. The trouble was that a lot of this information dealt with small areas and would not appeal to wider international readers. While selecting material, I have tried to avoid repetition and I hope that this mixed potpourri will spark off and/or widen the interest in a seriously neglected subject. The remains from the Second World War are fascinating and it is a pity that many relics are still being destroyed instead of being preserved as ancient monuments to become poignant reminders of our turbulent history. A few brilliant museums have been created, but many of them are struggling. They may have an abundance of material but not enough finances to preserve and display their collections. The Internet is a great help in finding these worthwhile heritage sites and most of them welcome volunteers to help bring the past to life again.

Some modern books now include Internet connections, but experience has shown that these can be out of date by the time the book goes on sale, and the links can then no longer be found. Therefore such connections have not been included in this book. However, a reasonable search engine should find many of the heritage / museum sites mentioned. Google and other maps with satellite views are also most useful.

A huge gun pit with sand camouflage at Ijmuiden (Holland).

CHAPTER 1
German Naval Bases

As a rough guide one can assume that at least ten men were required on land to support every sailor who went to sea. In addition to this there were a vast number of training establishments manned by naval personnel, a good number of coastal artillery units and many purely land-based support units wearing naval uniforms. Thus this land-based part of the navy, about which so little has been written, must have been enormous. Stories often become more involved the deeper one delves into local, rather than national, history. Therefore, when one dives even deeper, into personal and family history, one can easily get lost in an amazing maze of fascinating events that make it difficult to find a limit to one's studies.

Garmany's huge land-based naval organization was drastically reduced in size and power after the First World War, when the victorious Allies imposed what they called the Treaty of Versailles. This was not a negotiated treaty; the more polite Germans referred to it as the Versailles Dictate, while others looked upon it as a downright betrayal. It reduced the Reich to nothing more than a slave nation, unable to support itself. This state of affairs resulted in the majority of military installations being dismantled and many buildings standing empty. So, fifteen years later, when Hitler re-introduced national conscription, there were no great problems in finding accommodation.

The big crunch came when the Second World War forced the navy to expand far beyond national boundaries. Vast tracks of the continental coast had to be occupied to prevent Britain and France from using them as spring boards for attacks on the Reich. An incredibly long chain of harbours and defences was established, stretching from Norway's North Cape to the edge of the Sahara. There were bases along the shores of the Atlantic, the Mediterranean, on the Black Sea, and even as far away as the Indian Ocean and Pacific. These centres were manned by an ever-increasing number of men; the pressure to train them made it necessary for educational establishments to start looking for suitable additional accommodation in foreign countries.

The navy did not man all the foreign stations. Many of the coastal defences, often some distance from harbours but close to good landing beaches, were under army control, and others belonged to the Luftwaffe. The navy tended to place heavy artillery in locations where the main targets were likely to be fast moving ships rather than aircraft or assault forces wanting to land men ashore. In addition to this, not all of the defences in foreign

Until the end of the First World War, many coastal defence guns were located inside open-top pits with their barrels protruding above a protecting wall. This was often allowed to be overgrown by natural vegetation for camouflage purposes. The more sophisticated guns, as seen here, could be lowered behind the wall to be completely hidden from view until the moment of firing, making them exceedingly difficult for invading battleships to spot and hit. Such defences were amazingly effective until a single, small and rather flimsy aircraft could put them out of action by flying over the top with relatively tiny bombs. This meant that the entire fortification concept was drastically transformed during the First World War, when aircraft made their first serious appearance.

countries were established from scratch; existing installations were also modified for occupation by German forces.

Maintaining this massive network became a logistical nightmare and one wonders how one nation, with a comparatively small navy, managed to support such a widespread net, much of which had to be supplied from the homeland. One of the biggest problems for men in many of these locations was that nothing, absolutely nothing, ever happened in their vicinity. This meant that many of them became good fishermen, hunters, gardeners or farmers to dig for victory, if one is allowed to poach the British idiom. Despite many defences never firing a shot in anger, the First World War had shown that Britain did not shy away from the most audacious attacks; these lonely bastions had to be ready for the most unexpected surprises. For example, in April 1918, Britain attempted to block the canal leading from Zeebrugge (Belgium) to the German U-boat base in Brugge by sinking ships in its narrow channel. As a result, Germany had to mourn for eight dead and there were fourteen wounded. On the other side, the British force lost over 200 men and had almost 400 wounded, showing that a desperate enemy was prepared to sacrifice large numbers and expend considerable resources for hardly any gain. The gaps left between the sunken ships were wide enough for U-boats to pass through.

By the Second World War, such situations were made worse by there being enough narrow channels where aircraft, the new emerging weapon, could easily drop mines without being observed. The First World War problem of submarines mining deep-water shipping channels without being noticed was amplified considerably. In addition to this, there had been a number of other new inventions to change the thinking of the coastal defence networks. The most significant of these was presented by new and improved artillery. Modern guns could be aimed accurately over much longer distances, meaning that coastal defences had to be brought up to date; the bastions along lonely coasts became even more important parts of an essential network. It was quickly realized that these batteries were considerably cheaper than building large warships and that the functions of many smaller defence flotillas could be transferred to land-based concrete frigates. These land-based batteries became so prevalent in some regions, especially in Norway and along the Calais area of the English Channel, that the navy dispensed with heavily armoured ships.

Although some people think that the War brought coastal shipping to a near standstill, very much the opposite is true. A high proportion of the coastal communities depended on their sea routes. Isolated settlements, especially in Norway, produced their own meat, milk and potatoes, but they needed to import coal, fats, sugar and cereals. Indeed, this dependence of coastal trade stretched far inland and many essential industries would have ground to a halt had the coastal and river traffic been interrupted. Indeed some of the more isolated outposts could only be reached by ship or plane. In many cases there were neither long-distance, well-surfaced roads nor railways. The bigger, more central bases, where such connections had been built, found that the existing infrastructure of 1939 was not capable of satisfying the wartime demands. Additional roads and railway lines had to be built in considerable quantities.

Getting ships in or out of ports was relatively easy compared to the more exacting task of supporting traffic running parallel to the coast. The regulations for new recruits joining naval artillery may have been more lax than for sea-going personnel, but there certainly wasn't any room for soldiers lacking in initiative or drive. There might have been long periods of boredom, when nothing happened, but these men were called upon to perform the most dangerous and delicate juggling acts, and often keep up the momentum for long periods. For example, during the Channel Dash, when the battleships *Scharnhorst* and *Gneisenau* and the heavy cruiser *Prinz Eugen* ran from Brest in France to Germany, timing for minesweepers and escorts had to be correct to a few minutes and any deviation from ordered times could have resulted in catastrophic consequences. The start of the operation was delayed for a couple of hours due to a bombing raid and it was thought that even such a short period of time could be enough to destroy the coordinated plan. Many of the escorts, especially aircraft, accompanied the battle squadron only for

After the First World War many Germans were forced to live in extreme poverty, unable to feed themselves adequately, buy sufficient clothing or heat their homes during cruel winters. Power stations were often shut down for long periods because there was not enough fuel and many families had to do without electricity and gas as well as coal. Yet, despite this severe deprivation, foreign armies of occupation entered the industrial heartlands with guns at the ready to ensure that coal from German mines was forcibly exported as war reparations. The ill feelings and the hardships this created can hardly be described in words. This picture of the Kiel Naval Base is significant as it was taken shortly after the National Socialists came to power. They assured people that there would be work, food, clothing and heating for all workers. So, turning on the lights at night was not only functional but also a terrific morale booster, showing quite clearly that the country was being pulled out of the deepest and most horrifying recession. Perhaps it is no wonder that so many were keen to support the new order.

comparatively short distances, while it was passing through their immediate coastal waters, and the delay could have meant that small units had run out of fuel by the time they were required to guard the big ships. Getting such jobs done, often at exceedingly short notice and with ships that were difficult to identify, was not easy under those terrifying war conditions.

One strange point about German coastal fortifications is that the cost of this massive building programme was so enormous that it will probably never be calculated. Even if one looks at the huge U-boat shelters in isolation, one must wonder at the incredible expense of the undertaking. Yet, despite all this effort, sacrifice and hardship, Germany hardly provided the navy with a means of getting in and out of their own bastions, and many ships were sunk because adequate protection was not available once they were beyond the safety of the coast. To give just one example, the Norwegian freighter *Tirranna* was captured in the Indian Ocean in June 1940 by auxiliary cruiser *Atlantis*. Two months later the ship was filled with prisoners and provisions for a voyage of almost seven weeks. The prize crew took the ship as far as the Gironde Estuary in France only to be torpedoed by HM Submarine *Tuna* (Lieutenant Commander Cavanagh-Mainwaring) while waiting for escort into port. Two days later the same submarine hit the catapult ship *Ostmark*, a tiny aircraft mother ship of 1,281 tons. Karl Dönitz, the officer commanding the U-boat Arm was astonished and remarked that it won't be long before U-boats are going to be sunk on their own doorstep.

These days it is exceedingly difficult to establish the exact number of German naval bases and to work out precisely where they were located. Some of them were tiny and incredibly isolated. To reach them one had to travel to the end of a long, narrow and often deserted lane with the most appalling surface. Then, when it stopped, it was necessary to carry on a bit with the hope that one didn't get lost. In many cases, when one reached the outpost after a long day's travel along difficult paths, it was clear that one had started the journey only a few miles away, but a ferocious river with incredible currents barred the direct route. When trying to pinpoint such locations on a map, one quickly runs into problems. First, some places were so remote that the local names hardly feature in modern large-scale road atlases. Secondly, these little-known names were often Germanized in naval records and bear hardly any resemblance to the original. To make this even more confusing, some places were referred to by German codenames. While some of the names of towns or villages or headlands might be relatively easy to identify, there were others that referred to a piece of land not much bigger than a football field; trying to find that without local knowledge is virtually impossible. It is also surprising how popular some names are; it is not uncommon to find half a dozen places in the roughly the same area and all with almost the same name. In addition to this, after the War many name changes occurred, especially in German areas, which passed into foreign administration. Different names for the same place and post-war name changes make the hunt through old records most frustrating.

Such conundrums require considerable local knowledge, without which it is virtually impossible to find some of the more secret bases. Indeed, searching for old wartime locations can produce astonishing surprises because the names in German records often give no clue at all about size. A naval artillery unit, for example, could have been a single, small pit with a couple of guns among sand dunes, or a massive set of fortifications with well over a hundred powerful bunkers.

While bunkers built during the War clearly look like military installations, many of the earlier buildings were disguised to blend in with their surroundings. The U-boat headquarters at Sengwarden is a good example. From the air the complex was designed to look like a large farm; one of the main concrete communications bunkers in Wilhelmshaven has been hidden behind a veneer of bricks to resemble part of a large country estate.

Finding old bases is made more difficult by the fact that the majority of sea-going officers didn't know exactly where the main headquarters were. Of course, there is no reason why they should have known. Their main communication routes were radio, telex or telephone connections and very few actually needed to call at headquarters. When they did, they would have been taken by car because such buildings were often some distance from harbours. To make such locations even more mysterious, photography near these sites was prohibited and official war photographers had strict instructions to compose

Gardening and small-scale farming became an important activity of many land-based naval units and made a significant contribution to their existence. This picture shows part of the naval base in Kiel converted by the 5th U-boat Flotilla to make best use of leftovers from the messes.

their pictures in such a manner that easily recognized landmarks would not reveal any locations.

Some bunkers have had their foundations undermined by the sea and have tumbled into the water. Many others along the shores from Holland to the north of Denmark have fallen foul to wandering sand dunes. Wind-blown sand has buried them and then marram grass has helped to bind the covering in place. Of course, this state of affairs has certain advantages and some of the sites still contain enough hardware to kit out an entire army; that is if the soldiers don't mind a bit of rust. The coastal batteries especially were surrounded by extensive mine entanglements, meaning no one could go near them until sometime after the War, when experts had removed the explosives. That means it is difficult to establish what the evacuating troops left behind and anyone searching for relics should bear in mind that live bombs, mines and all manner of other dangerous explosives still turn up regularly. During a six-week-long search for war relics along the English south coast, the author found four live bombs on three different occasions. It is also important to bear in mind that it is very easy to get into some bunkers, but exceedingly difficult or even impossible to climb out again without the right equipment or outside help.

German naval administration did not always take national boundaries into account and a wartime commander in France could well have been responsible for men in Holland. In any case, geographical locations were divided into three different ways and the divisions used by the Fleet Command differed slightly from the Security Forces, which again differed from the Coastal Defence Regions. Knowledge of the German administrative support network is not likely to help many modern researchers. Therefore it seems superfluous to provide such details in this book. It will be less confusing to classify the bases according to their modern nationality, rather than in the wartime administration pattern.

CHAPTER 2
Different Types of German Naval Bases

SMALL, ISOLATED BASES WITHOUT A PERMANENT NAVAL REPRESENTATIVE

The Remotest of All – the U-Places

The most remote and least-used type of base has got to be one of the secret anchorages mentioned in the naval list of U-Plätze or U-Places. Although this has been translated as having had something to do with U-boats, the 'U' stands for 'Unterkunft' (Accommodation). This highly secret list was compiled after the First World War to provide basic information about isolated but comparatively safe anchorages where both merchant and warships might take refuge in the event of an emergency. Many of these places were surveyed only by small expeditions and the details of some locations were determined by word-of-mouth from seafarers who happened to have visited them. Officialdom made a point of not showing a great deal of interest in these locations and basic navigational information was often lacking because the waters had not been charted properly. Therefore all ships could expect to find were sheltered areas a long way from prying eyes where minor repairs might be undertaken.

Even some spots officially charted by German expeditions were found to have some undiscovered death traps built into them. For example, shortly after the turn of the twentieth century, the light cruiser *Gazelle* charted several large, concealed bays of the Kerguelen Islands, but failed to find that one of the narrow entrances was guarded by a sharp rock hidden below the surface of the water. During the Second World War the auxiliary cruiser *Atlantis* lurched onto this pike in such a manner that it pierced the outer hull of a fresh-water tank and then held the ship firmly in place. None of the usual emergency manoeuvres pulled the ship free and even a diver's description didn't satisfy the commander, Kpt.z.S. Bernhard Rogge. Despite never having dived before, he donned on the gear and investigated the problem himself before ordering the crew to carry all heavy objects from the punctured area to the other end of the ship to create an artificial list. It was several days before the converted freighter could be pulled free again.

The vast majority of harbour protection boats were converted fishing boats, tugs or something of a similar nature. One could distinguish them by a large web-like radio aerial strung between the masts and often with an elevated lookout and searchlight. This boat is obviously employed by the military because it has a gun on the bows and minesweeping gear can be identified on the stern. Although such harbour protection boats or patrol boats may have looked like heaps of rust, they acquired that appearance because they spent so much time at sea, often in the most appalling conditions when it would be inappropriate to have men on deck for anything other than essential duties.

Many fishing boats commandeered by the navy kept their earlier civilian crews for two reasons. First, the navy did not have the manpower to man the vast number of ships being drawn into war service, and secondly, the majority of naval sailors would not have coped with the wild idiosyncrasies of such small craft. Such civilian crews would have had a naval officer as commander and there would have been a number of military specialists for dealing with the highly technical nature of their weapons.

Escape and Survival Bases

The second grade of base was an unmanned escape location, situated mainly on lonely Arctic islands. The initial plan was to hide survival items for meteorological crews and airmen of the weather flights, who might be forced to make emergency landings. The Luftwaffe prepared a number of emergency landing strips and then equipped these with essential survival aids. Suitable ground was often determined by merely dropping large round boulders out of the bomb bay; if they bounced, then a team of ground preparers was parachuted down with ample provisions. These volunteers moved rocks out of the way until there was enough space to land an aircraft. Some U-boats and special Arctic trawlers helped in setting up such bases as well, but many of these facilities were intended more for Luftwaffe weather flights and for the meteorological service rather than for the navy. The reason for this was that the water temperatures were so low that the chances of surviving a sinking were pretty remote and shipwrecked sailors were unlikely to make their way to any of these out-of-the-way places.

The survival aids for such locations, including tinned food, were usually packed in boxes lined with waxed paper. Hot wax was poured over the packaging before everything was sealed inside a wooden box. These boxes were designed to stack sideways so that the lids would serve as doors. This made it possible to use the boxes for building a wall around a tent or hut to provide extra protection from the weather. Once in location, stones were usually piled around the outside to hide them from view, but also to make the dump obvious for someone who didn't know exactly where it was. Some of these dumps were equipped with enough necessities, including pistols and hunting weapons, to keep a number of men alive for several months.

Automatic, Unmanned Radio Stations

A number of these were established in the Arctic, mainly for transmitting weather data to a German receiver. The navy installed the majority, but the Luftwaffe also set up some. There were land-based automatic weather reporting stations and the navy also used a floating variety, which could be assembled aboard a U-boat and then dropped over the side. The land-based varieties were disadvantageous as they were prone to freezing solid, and therefore ceasing to work. Almost of all of these must have vanished by now, with many having fallen foul to curious hunters who smashed them. Such stations were set up in several Arctic locations as far away as Greenland and Canada. In fact the Canadian station was not re-discovered until many years after the War when the Coast Guard helped in bringing parts back to civilization for display in a museum.

Small Manned Weather Stations

Although naval personnel did not man many of these, a good number were installed by small boats or by submarines and some of them were large enough to warrant a U-boat having to make two journeys in order to set up one base. Setting up usually took place towards the end of the year, when rough weather and ice made it difficult for the enemy to attack the location. The crew was then evacuated before the melting ice of the following year provided access for enemy warships. As has already been mentioned,

Even small ports could well have had a number of torpedo and anti-submarine nets as can be seen here on the extreme left. Bow thrusters and other modern docking aids had not yet been invented for the Second World War, therefore tugs were always required to help big ships in and out of harbours, even during calm conditions. Although there were naval tugs, the vast majority were manned by local crews who knew the quirks of the sea where they lived.

these huts also had a number of escape routes in case a raiding party surprised the crews.

SMALL NAVAL BASES WITH A PERMANENT NAVAL REPRESENTATIVE

Bases with a Harbour Master or Port Commander

The smallest permanent naval harbour was one with a harbour master or a port commander. A harbour master (Hafenkapitän) could have been a civilian, while a port commander (Hafenkommandant) was nearly always a naval officer; this latter version was used more often towards the end of the War. (Note that although the Germans used the term 'Kommandant' for someone in charge of a ship or boat and 'Kommandeur' for commanders of land-based units, they still used the title of Hafenkommandant for port commanders.)

Civilian harbour masters would have come under military jurisdiction once the War started and even before the War they would have been 'Beamte' or civil servants, who could look forward to a reasonable pension once they retired. The downside of the job was that any damage caused by their negligence would have had to be paid for by the employee, and there were cases where the pension used as collateral to pay for mishaps.

Good sea-going experience aboard either merchant or warships was an important prerequisite for such positions, but that was no great problem during the 1930s. Air travel hardly existed and transporting goods and passengers by sea was still a major industry with an incredibly huge workforce. So there were no problems finding seafarers to fill such prestigious and sought-after land-based positions.

Harbour masters and port commanders would have had a considerable staff, including a secure radio station. Even bigger locations, where telephone cables could also carry telex lines, would have had such a radio office as backup in case the telephone wires were cut during emergencies. Telex was a forerunner of the fax system, enabling one typewriter-like machine to send written messages to another. Each machine had a dial for making contact with other machines and the messages typed on one machine were printed out on paper by the machine at the destination.

A harbour master would have had at least a few small boats and a sizeable staff of guards, drivers, a quartermaster, a few secretaries, a cook; even a minor location required a number of people to run it efficiently. The main duties were to supply weather details, tidal information, soundings measuring water depth and any special precautions required to enter the harbour. The harbour master would allocate moorings and ensure that everything under his jurisdiction was safe and in best running order. Communication with ships at sea would have been either by telephone from the ships' last port, giving an approximate time of arrival, or by radio if they were already at sea. In addition to this, virtually all the main ports also had visual reporting stations with which ships could make contact if their radios were not working. It was often essential to obtain permission to enter a port before coming within range of its defensive guns; the crews manning these batteries did not always wait for orders before engaging suspicious ships. In some isolated places, a remote gun battery might have doubled up as visual signal station.

The boundaries of a harbour master's jurisdiction were not always clear and serious disputes were relatively frequent. One of the major problems lay in dealing with local shipping in foreign waters. On the one hand, this was essential to keep the complicated system working, but on the other it made life more than difficult, especially where small boats were allowed to ply their trade close to a military base. A high proportion of the men manning these small boats were not aware of international regulations, having grown up doing what they wanted, rather than learning rules from books. The worst offenders were fishermen, who tended twist and turn their boats in order to follow the fish, often without a great deal of regard to other users of the shipping channels. In addition to this, they continued as they had done before the War, when their hunting grounds were often devoid of other ships and it was not necessary to mark their nets clearly. Locals would have known where each fisherman had his nets, but foreign sailors trained in naval academies were not always taught such intricacies. U564 under Teddy Suhren cut across one such net, which wrapped tightly around the propellers. The U-boat drifted for several hours before the crew was able to disentangle the twisted mess. Harbour masters were often blamed for such accidents, with the victims saying that local shipping should not be allowed anywhere near the military routes.

A Harbour Protection Flotilla (Hafenschutzflottille) would have had an officer as flotilla commander; a port with such a group would also have had a harbour master, although this has been omitted from the list in this book to avoid repetition. Large naval bases had a variety of well-armed vessels, some of them with highly specialized weapons,

This pass for the Naval Dockyard in Wilhelmshaven, made out for the Apprentice Heinz Steinmetz, is now on display at the International Maritime Museum in Hamburg. On top of it are two lapel badges for shipyard workers: the Achievement Badge for Shipyard Workers (Werftleistungs-abzeichen) on the left and a Wilhelmshaven Shipyard Badge on the right. Getting into shipyards was a basic necessity for many escaped prisoners of war if they wanted to stow away on a ship bound for a neutral country. Copying passes for ordinary docks was sometimes possible because many were nothing more than a typewritten sheet of paper. However, forging a pass like this, for a naval dockyard, would have been very difficult for the majority of people.

but smaller bases had to make do with an assortment of makeshift boats, many of them converted fishing trawlers or even drifters. Life on them would have been uncomfortable and the crews often had their main accommodation on land rather than on board. Many of these boats would have put to sea for only comparatively short periods of a maximum of a few days at a time. Yet they performed vital duties in keeping the sea-lanes open and free from mines.

Roads running around some harbours were often in poor states of repair and difficult to negotiate, so it was likely that some bases had a fleet of small ferries providing an essential 'bus or taxi' service between the main centres. It was quite likely that some minesweepers were not permanently based in one port, but would escort ships through coastal waters for longer journeys. There were also a number of coastal protection flotillas, made up of bigger, sea-going vessels which could be moved from one hot spot to another, although they tended to remain within their own operations area and hardly proceeded far beyond it. Their duty was to escort lone ships or convoys through coastal waters.

THE MAIN NAVAL BASE

At the most important end of the naval command spectrum was a Main Naval Base commanded by an admiral. The most important part of this would have been a naval dockyard, which was also headed by an admiral. Before the War his title would have been Oberwerftdirektor (Chief Shipyard Director). This was later changed to Werftkommandant (Shipyard Commander). His main duty was to ensure all ships were in the best possible condition and that all his land-based departments were functioning to their ultimate capacity.

After the end of the First World War, Germany was left with only one functioning Naval Base at Wilhelmshaven, although the Allies removed many of the valuable fittings, including cranes, floating dry docks and other heavy ship construction gear. The Naval Dockyards in Kiel and in Danzig were disbanded and Kiel was downgraded to a mere base with a naval arsenal. The following is a list of the main naval offices, departments and sections in Wilhelmshaven towards the beginning of the Second World War as an example to show what a major dockyard contributed to keep the fleet at sea. These departments came under the jurisdiction of the backup or organisation side of the navy and none of the operational units based in the port have been included in this list.

North Sea Naval Station (Marinestation der Nordsee) based in Wilhelmshaven, later Supreme Naval Command of the North Sea (Marineoberkommando der Nordsee)

'Ressort' translates as 'department' or 'area of responsibility'.

Supreme Director of Dockyard	Oberwerftdirektor
Aide de camp	Adjutant
Chief of Dockyard Staff	Chef des Stabes
Central (Administration) Department	Zentralabteilung
Dockyard Director's Staff	Stabsoffiziere beim Stabe
Dockyard Management	Werftleitung
Operations and Planning Office	Betriebs und Planungsamt
Equipment and Navigation Department	Ausrüstungs & Navigationsressort
Artillery (later: Weapons) Department	Artillerieressort / Waffenabteilung
Construction Department	Schiffsbauressort

Marine Engine Production Department	Maschinenbauressort
Port Construction Department	Hafenbauressort
Underwater Construction Department	Strombauressort
Navigation Department	Navigationsressort
Torpedo Department	Torpedoressort
Mine Department	Minenressort
Communication Equipment Department	Nachrichtenmittelressort
Supplies Department	Nachschubressort
Administration Department	Verwaltungsressort
Personnel Office	Arbeiteramt
Dockyard Medical Services	Werftoberarzt
Dockyard Hospital	Werftkrankenhaus
Remote Control Unit	Fernlenkverband

Commanding Admiral later Supreme Commander-in-Chief of the North Sea Naval Station (Kommandierender Admiral / Oberbefehlshaber der Marinestation der Nordsee)

Admiral's Staff Department: Main Offices	Admiralstabs~abteilung: Main Offices
1st Admiral's Staff Officer	1. Admiralstabsoffizier
2nd Admiral's Staff Officer	2. Admiralstabsoffizier
3rd Admiral's Staff Officer	3. Admiralstabsoffizier
4th Admiral's Staff Officer	4. Admiralstabsoffizier
Defence Officer	Abwehroffizier
Shipping Adviser	Schiffahrtsreferent
Air Raid Adviser	Luftschutzreferent
Public Relations Officer	Presseoffizier
Station Engineer	Stationsingenieur
Medical Officer	Sanitätsoffizier
Administration Officer	Stationsverwaltungsoffizier
Engineer / Construction Officer	Pionieroffizier
Welfare Officer	Wehrbetreuungsoffizier
Library	Bücherei
Printed Papers Administration	Druckschriftenverwaltung
Naval Officer Personnel Department	Marineoffizierspersonalabteilung
Personnel Office	Personal oder Gefolgschaftsamt
Judiciary	Rechtsabteilung

Other Offices:	
Physiological Testing Authority	Psychologische Prüfstelle
Pilot and Sea Marking Command	Lotsenkommando/Seezeichenamt
Naval Communications Department	Marinenachrichtenabteilung
Naval Direction Finding Department	Marinepeilabteilung

Military Communications Command	Wehrmachtsnachrichtenkommandantur
Naval Observatory	Marineobservatorium
Naval Convalescence Home	Marinekurheim
Home Administration	Heimatverwaltung
Naval Pay Office	Marinebesoldungsstelle
2nd Admiral of the North Sea	2. Admiral der Nordsee
Chief of Staff	Chef des Stabes
Court with Presiding Judge	Dienstaufsichtsrichter
Personnel Department	Personalabteilung
Recruitment Officer	Einstellungsoffizier
Medical Department	Sanitätsabteilung
Administration Department	Verwaltungsabteilung
Crew Training Divisions	Schiffstammeinheiten
Naval Reserve Regiment	Marineersatzregiment
Warship Training Department	Ausbildungsabteilung Kriegsschiffe
Transport Department	Transportabteilung
Construction Standing-By Department	Marinebaubereitschaftsabteilung
Female Naval Auxiliaries Department	Marinehelferinnenersatzabteilung
Naval Administration School	Marineverwaltungsschule

Bearing in mind that the above includes only the main core of departments found in Wilhelmshaven, it is not too difficult to double the number of official establishments in one naval base. This intricate system was mirrored in Kiel, where there were even more command and support offices.

Units under the Fleet Command, U-boats, Security Forces and other operational groups have not been included. Obviously, this massive organizational pattern was drastically diluted when setting up bases in foreign countries.

FUNCTIONS OF THE MAIN LAND-BASED NAVAL DEPARTMENTS

The function of some departments is fairly obvious and therefore explanations have been omitted.

Marinearsenal

Marinearsenal did not necessarily mean a store for weapons and ammunition, although supplying such items was part of the duties. The term came into more everyday usage after the end of the First World War, when the Imperial Naval Dockyards in Kiel and Danzig had to be dissolved. Danzig was then demilitarized, but the naval dockyard remnants in Kiel remained operational under the new name of Marinearsenal. The term was later used for larger naval dockyards in foreign countries that did not have full-blown naval dockyard facilities.

Administration Department (Verwaltungsressort)

This department was expected to supply both personnel and materials likely to be required to keep every other branch under their jurisdiction operational. Materials included everything from food, fuel for road vehicles, furniture, building materials, books for libraries and anything else that was likely to be required. Although often looked down upon by sea-going personnel, not much would have happened had it not been for efficient administration departments.

Equipment Department (Ausrüstungsressort)

The main aim of this department was to provide all naval ships, no matter what command they came from, with fuel, lubricating oil, water and any other necessities needed to keep them operational. In the absence of other harbour authorities, this department was also responsible for ensuring a safe passage into the port, providing the necessary quay space and any auxiliary vessels, such as tugs, required for docking. Once docked, this department would provide the necessary official transport for crews of in-coming units. This was especially important where command centres were some distance from the harbour and the in-coming unit's officers needed to consult urgently with higher authorities. Off-duty sailors were expected to use public transport, although bus or boat shuttle services were sometimes provided. The Equipment Department was also expected to maintain a large enough staff to ensure that whatever was issued to ships was of the correct quality. This was especially important as far as different grades of fuel, lubricating oils and greases for different ships were concerned.

Ship Construction and Marine Engines Department (Schiffsbauressort und Maschinenbauressort)

This department was responsible for the technical repair and management of ships, propulsion units and the electrical backup required to make everything work properly. Experts were expected to be on hand to help with any technical problem that might arise. Again, the larger ships would have had enough staff to cope with quite serious problems, while smaller boats often had to make do with less qualified people.

Many technical officers in smaller ships came to the navy as a result of the emergency war programme and often lacked the detailed education required to deal properly with highly technical aspects beyond their daily duties. This was one field where disputes and problems often occurred. For example, Kptlt. Heinrich Driver recorded in U371's log that when he put into Brest before becoming the first boat to enter the Mediterranean, he reported for the second time that the sound detector was not working properly. Following a test by dockyard staff the engineer officer of U371 was told that the system was in perfect electrical order. Kptlt. Heinrich Driver made the point that as commander he should have had the power to overrule such a ridiculous dockyard bureaucracy because with five years experience he could determine whether such equipment was functioning or not. The dockyard experts may have found the circuits to be in working order, but the gear didn't work properly. He felt deeply peeved at having to do without this essential aid during such a difficult voyage.

Gripes like these were frequently recorded in logbooks and tend to give the impression that the backup system of the German Navy didn't function terribly well, which is not true. There have been several incidents where men involved in such disputes were interviewed after the War and then laughed about the matter, saying it was just one minor isolated point, created by a misunderstanding. Generally they were more than pleased with the support they received from naval dockyards. In fact, after the War no one criticised any dockyard workers and many interviewees went out of their way to praise their high standards.

Port Construction Department (Hafenbauressort)

This department was responsible for maintaining harbour installations, both below and above the waterline, to ensure they were adequate for the tasks in hand and safe for use. Many harbours were too small to maintain such departments, meaning that teams of experts travelled from one port to another, establishing exactly what remedial work needed to be carried out. This was especially important in foreign bases, where the standard of harbour installations was often far below the standard expected in Germany. Even large ports such as Trondheim in Norway did not meet German safety standards and considerable remedial work had to be put in hand. However, the health and safety regulations were not as silly as they are today, where many rules seem to have been established for making the controlling industry richer rather than for providing a safer working environment. Even unsafe facilities continued to be used during wartime, but then the men working there were made aware of the dangers so that extra care could be taken.

The following example has been provided to give some idea of the type of work carried out by Port Construction Departments. This work was carried out in south and central Norway during a period of six months leading up to the end of October 1940.

Explosives were used on more than 100,000 occasions to clear obstructions, consuming over 30,000 tons of explosives.

The following were consumed during these projects:
9,000 tons of cement
45,000 tons of hardcore, consisting mainly of shingle and gravel
642 tons of iron
23,000 tons of timber

This was used to build:
300 metres of piers in almost 30 locations
7,000 metres of new huts / buildings were erected
23 wells were dug
50 kilometres of new water pipelines were laid
100 kilometres of new electric cables were put in place, some on pylons
40 kilometres of new roads were built
30 kilometres of old roads were improved so that they could carry lorries

Navigation Department (Navigationsressort)

The main aim was to predict and supply all navigation materials, which were likely to be asked for in any area. This included charts, nautical handbooks and navigation equipment; all of this had to be supplied in such a manner that it could be used aboard ships with the poorest facilities. Some charts, for example, had to be printed on water-resistant paper. The hardware included spare parts for things like magnetic and gyrocompasses, clocks, barometers and barographs, sextants, gyro sextants and thermometers. This became so intricate that the department was further divided into five specialist sections to ensure the right equipment and up-to-date charts were available at all times. Details of German and foreign minefields were especially important as some of these details changed during a single war voyage.

Communications Equipment Unit (Nachrichtenmittelbetrieb)

This department was responsible for maintaining radios on ships and both radios and landlines for land-based units. The department should have provided spare parts for most of the common equipment and experts to deal with any problems radio operators could not cope with on their own. This equipment included the main official communications networks aboard ships, radios for listening to public broadcasts, record players, radar equipment, radar detectors and coding machines.

Artillery Department (Artillerieressort)

This department was responsible for maintaining all guns from the largest aboard ships to the smallest handguns. Generally facilities included weapons up to a size found on the majority of smaller ships – about 105 mm. Large cruisers, battleships and the like would have had their own specialist staff to deal with heavy weapons unique to the ship. It was also quite likely that specialist weapons such as torpedoes and mines for U-boats, torpedo boats and destroyers, had their own supply base in harbours where such units called regularly.

Torpedo Department (Torpedoressort)

The naval dockyard often supplied torpedoes, but special torpedo arsenals were created later during the War. It is strange that although most of the torpedoes seem to have been of standard type, the important means of carrying them by crane was left to be sorted out by the men loading them. One would have thought that the navy had also developed a special cradle type of belt for holding them on cranes, but in old photos one sees a mass of different methods for attaching these valuable missiles to hooks and wires.

Dockyard Medical Service

As far as possible the navy avoided sending ill or injured men to civilian hospitals and made every effort to provide the best medical facilities available. This included the providing of medical check ups for men coming from and going on operational voyages, seeing to teeth and dealing with other ailments that might arise in special locations. There

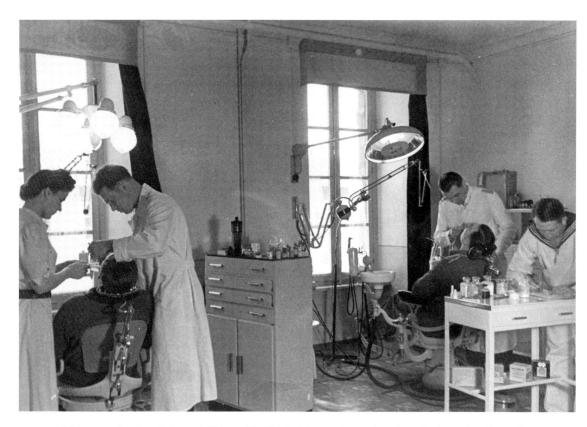

The naval dentist of the 11th U-boat Flotilla in Norway. Dental and medical services formed a vital part of all the major naval bases. Larger warships would have had their own facilities with impressively high standards of service, but the vast majority of men had to make use of the facilities in the ports. Dental services were still very much in their infancy, but one of the main culprits for tooth decay, sugar, was not so plentiful until long after the Second World War. Despite this, the condition of teeth was one of the main stumbling blocks for joining the more selective branches of the armed forces and many men were turned away because their teeth were no longer in prime condition by the time they left school or finished their apprenticeship.

were a number of specialist sections dealing with specific issues such as the health aboard U-boats.

Personnel Office (Personalamt or the older term Gefolgschaftsamt)

This was an incredibly difficult department to organize and run because it had to deal with many different nationalities and take foreign customs, currencies and beliefs into consideration. What is more, some employees had their wages paid into two separate accounts, one for the worker and another for his family back home. Employing workers, terminating their contracts and determining their wages was usually carried out at a central office rather than by a naval station in a foreign country. Some employees came via the Todt Organisation rather than the naval administration. This department was mainly responsible for the wellbeing of all employees and looked after the majority of

Naval authorities were fully aware that sailors were cooped up in exceptionally cramped conditions for unnaturally long periods and such a state of affairs could easily lead to bodies and minds becoming dangerously lethargic. The photograph of this naval gymnasium is of special interest because it shows that the men made do without the fancy and highly expensive machinery found in modern health centres. What's more the floor is covered with nothing more sophisticated than a thick layer of sand to soften any falls. Yet despite the pre-war gymnasiums being much simpler, they did help in producing healthier people than are generally seen today. The gymnastic skills of some sailors of the Second World War era were surprisingly high and it was not uncommon for visitors watching displays in Britain and in Germany to think that a random group of ordinary sailors were part of a special display team. The interesting point about much of this physical activity was that the men were often not forced to take part, but volunteered to try out the most amazing acts in the tightly confined spaces of warships.

their needs, including finding accommodation, feeding them, seeing that they had suitable clothing and so forth.

Workers at naval bases generally received more favourable wages than what private firms in the area would have paid them, and many were supplied with their daily needs by the German state. The vast majority of these foreign or guest workers were volunteers and for much of the War there was no shortage coming forward to fill vacant posts. What is more, many of these foreign workers produced better results than their counterparts in Germany. For example, German dockyard workers required one third longer to turn a U-boat around than their French counterparts. The rich flow of foreign workers appearing to volunteer for the German forces slowed considerably as a result of the massive bombing attacks on the bases; towards the end of the War there was a noticeable increase in the number of sabotage attempts.

Sefton Delmer, one of the key leaders of the British Political Warfare Executive, wrote

Part of the minesweeper depot in Bordeaux (France). The problem with maintaining naval bases was that no one could foretell what was likely to be required, so the supply divisions had to be ready for every eventuality and keep an adequate stock of items which were likely to be lost at sea. In addition to this, equipment had to be maintained in prime condition and stock checks were a regular part of the routine. This shows the paravane store for minesweepers.

in his fascinating book (see Bibliography) that contrary to the propaganda made up by his own department, he didn't believe that the majority of foreign workers were forced to work for Germany. He saw them more as willing collaborators, attracted by the good wages and the good conditions offered to them by Germany.

Remote Control Unit

This unit appears here because it was originally part of the Naval Dockyard in Wilhelmshaven and it was not until the summer of 1942 that an independent Remote Control Unit was created. The old battleships *Zähringen* and *Hessen* and the later the light cruiser *Königsberg* plus a few smaller ships such as *T151* and *T185* (T = Torpedo Boat) were converted to run without anyone on board so that they could be used as targets for heavy artillery. The superstructure was greatly modified to look like a hulk with rectangular boxes on top, so that there was no danger of a dim-witted artillerist shooting at passing ships.

The Second Admiral

This was not an operational but and organizational position and consisted of a vast setup to keep the fleet provisioned and fully operational. Keeping the navy supplied with a steady flow of trained recruits was one of the major contributions made by the Second Admiral. Men usually joined the navy either under the Baltic or North Sea Naval Commands and quickly learned that there were not only traditions but also some strong friendly rivalry separating the two. Although the sailors may have looked alike to the average landlubber, there were subtle differences in the way they wore their uniforms. The most obvious being the diagonal line of the scarf had a different orientation depending on whether the sailor belonged to the Baltic or North Sea Commands. His military number would also have been prefixed with either 'O' (Baltic is Ostsee in German) or 'N'.

Men who joined the German armed forces first had to go through a period of initial training. In the navy this was done with a naval infantry unit, while the men were kitted out in land-based uniforms. It was not until this had been completed and a military oath had been sworn that the men were allowed to wear naval uniform. The coming of war and the great demands on men meant that the neither of the two naval commands could cope with the pressure and newly formed initial training establishments were quickly moved out into foreign lands. This was relatively easy because there was no great need to have special equipment. Therefore training establishments could be set up with old weapons or even dummy weapons in any suitable building after a quick conversion, such as redundant factories, schools or existing military barracks.

CHAPTER 3

The Main Naval Bases
in Germany

WILHELMSHAVEN (MAIN NORTH SEA BASE)

The first Geographical Handbook released by the British Naval Intelligence Division after the Second World War stated that Wilhelmshaven is approached from the North Sea by a winding channel of the River Jade. The depth of water was liable to change dramatically owing to shifting sands, and most important of all, local knowledge was usually essential when approaching the port. A hundred years earlier, when the German Navy was founded during a war between Denmark and Prussia, Wilhelmshaven didn't exist yet. What is more, at that time it was almost impossible to approach the German North Sea coast from the water or from the land. In fact, in those days hardly anyone knew exactly where the coast was. The variation between high and low tide was (and still is) enormous, with unstable tidal salt marshes covering many tens of miles between shallow (waist deep) open water and firm land. Even that firm land was too soft for much of the year to carry heavy traffic, and if it were not for some ferocious currents, the water was shallow enough for non-swimming children to paddle in.

There were only a few isolated communities in that inhospitable belt, each dependent on a dyke thrown around a slightly raised mound. Most of these low hills started as natural sandbanks and were then made firmer by wind-blown sand being bound in place by marram grass. Others, especially the higher ones, were remnants from when ice age glaciers deposited impressive hills along stretches of the North Sea coast. In some cases the mounds were completely man-made by piling layers of sand, clay and cow dung on top of each other. It was not until Hitler came to power that a national government made a positive contribution by taking the responsibility for coastal defences away from small local communities to create a national coast protection scheme.

Even this mammoth effort by thousands of men was not able to withstand the incredible high water of the winter of 1962, and consequently another vast coastal defence scheme got underway. This has already proved its worth by holding firm against several even higher storms than the one that sparked off this tremendous new programme. Today, where the coast is well defined by a dyke running from Denmark as far as Holland, the area on the seaward side of these defences still remains part of Europe's wildest and most unpredictable frontier. Known in English under its Dutch name of Wadden Sea, it is vast. At high tide the water laps against a sandy beach in front of the dyke in Cuxhaven and at low tide the nearest non-dredged water is almost 20 kilometres further out in the North Sea, making it possible to walk as far as the infamous Scharhörn. This treacherous sandbank is still so active that many wrecks there are buried naturally and anyone going there should do so only with a local guide.

While the shifting low-tide route to Scharhörn is made up of fairly firm sand, the dead-end channels elsewhere tend to collect soft mud and in some places one can find deadly quicksands. The approaches to Wilhelmshaven have these rather sticky properties, but the site had to be chosen as Germany's main naval base because that is the only place along the entire coast where a deep-water channel runs close to what could be made into firm land once dyked. The rivers running into the North Sea were too unpredictable and too often clogged by sand or by commercial shipping. For example Stade, a small town on the banks of the River Elbe, about halfway between the estuary and the main port of Hamburg, once had a busy commercial harbour until a heavy inland storm brought so much sand that it was no longer possible for ships to sail in and out. Yet it seems highly likely that only a few years earlier Rear Admiral Horatio Nelson sailed in a scheduled package boat from Stade to Great Yarmouth.

All of Wilhelmshaven town was a Victorian creation, having been built initially between 1855 and 1869 and then more less continuously enlarged and modified. The land was originally polder, reclaimed from the sea by building a long dyke to enclose town and harbour. It still is less than 2 metres above mean sea level and the average water at neap tides rises to 3.5 metres and to almost 4 metres at higher tides. Thus the town would flood if the sea defences were to break. The water level in Wilhelmshaven's floating harbour or wet dock was maintained by a series of locks. This artificial, non-tidal stretch of water is about 6 kilometres long, has four major basins and many more specialised quays around its perimeter. Getting across this massive expanse was a major challenge and could at first be accomplished by passenger ferry, which also carried bicycles. The modern dam carrying a road across the western basin was not built until after the Second World War. Most impressive of all and not sparing any expense, Prussia also built the biggest swing bridge of the time at the eastern end to carry all manner of road traffic from one side to the other. This incredible structure is still fully operational today. However, in those early days when the bridge was built, there was little demand for crossing the harbour to what was largely nothing more than a sea dyke on the other side, but workmen attending to the sea defences and to the locks had to cross it regularly. There were also ferry terminals on the barren seaward side.

Getting ships in and out of this non-tidal harbour has always been a major problem. The navy have always required priority in the use of locks, meaning that a number of external basins, with a depth of just over 3 metres, were developed for local commercial use. These tidal moorings were attached to floating pontoons, which could rise and fall with the tides, although the rather exposed position makes them a little unpleasant in stormy weather. Wilhelmshaven never had a significant commercial harbour, mainly because there were no noteworthy consumer industries and most of the trade was in form of imports to supply both town and naval dockyard. Cargo ships were then unloaded in one of the specialised harbour basins. The outside tidal facilities were more for small boats and ferries running across the huge bay to Bremerhaven and to the Friesian islands.

Even today, where much of the former splendour has either disappeared or been fossilised, one can see that Prussia did not skimp when it came to developing this major North Sea base. Splendid buildings were supported by wide, pleasant roads and by a more than adequate rail connection. There was a main line running into a most imposing wooden station and a number of side loops for other commercial purposes. One of the most significant of these was a huge coaling station, supplying both the navy and merchants in town. Almost all the heating and most of the cooking stoves were initially coal-fired. The quays of the floating harbour were supplied with good rail connections, making it possible to reach almost every part. An airport was also added later, but this was initially purely a military facility because the average people could not have afforded to travel by air.

The locks of the floating harbour were numbered from left to right as one looked at them from the tidal side. However, the oldest pair, known as Entrance II, was already too small by the end of the nineteenth century and fell into disuse. They were then filled in and incorporated into the dyke. By the Second World War, Entrance III provided the main route in and out until the new, huge Raeder Locks were added during the middle of the War and now provide the only way in and out of the floating harbour. However, the present-day locks are not the same as those built earlier. The entire locking system, including a barrier capable of shutting off the dock basin from high storm tides, were destroyed after the Second World War when the British government planned on ripping out the high water defences as well so that the town would flood with every high tide. Luckily local protests prevented this insane act of destruction, although much of the harbour was destroyed after the War and was re-built after the army of occupation left.

Entrance III could cope with ships up to 250 metres in length and with a beam of 37.8 metres and a draught of 10 metres. One great disadvantage with such huge locks is that they consume a lot of power and it takes a long time for pumps to run through a complete cycle of raising the water level. This is much too slow for the modern navy and many of its ships are now berthed in a tidal pool below the locks, rather than in the floating harbour above them.

Wilhelmshaven could provide every facility ships might require and even boasted of its own fully fledged shipyard, where imposing giants such as pocket battleships *Admiral Graf Spee*, *Admiral Scheer* and the mighty battleship *Tirpitz* were built. Initially Germany had three naval ship building yards: in Danzig, Kiel and Wilhelmshaven. Two of them were closed after the First World War and Wilhelmshaven was ravaged and looted to such an extent that there were serious concerns during the early 1920s whether the facilities would ever again be capable of building large ships. Initial trials were made with small projects. Not only had the victorious Allies removed much of the heavy machinery, but the depravation created by the War and the appalling conditions immediately after it

The old engineers' barracks in Wilhelmshaven were among the first to be built when the naval base was established there during the heyday of steam. It was also one of the first to fall foul to bombs during the Second World War. The site was cleared so that a substantial air raid shelter could be built upon it.

The remains of the old engineers' barracks in Wilhelmshaven with a Second World War high bunker (Hochbunker) occupying the site bombed early in the War.

drove away the skilled labour that had not been called up for military service. So it was not only a case of re-building the infrastructure but also re-creating a highly specialised workforce. Then the first major challenge was the light cruiser *Emden*, which was launched in 1925. By the beginning of the Second World War there were a number of huge dry docks capable of holding the biggest battleships and three major floating cranes with a capacity of 250, 100 and 40 tons.

The four major basins of the floating harbour also supported a specialised torpedo arsenal at the far end and Germany's first purpose-built U-boat base. Although the U-boat Arm was originally established in Kiel before the First World War, there was never any room there for a dedicated base and the new U-boat flotillas had to fit in wherever there was space. In 1935, when the second generation of U-boats were being built in Kiel, the navy also started developing a special submarine base on a rather peaceful stretch of

Despite the new naval base at Wilhelmshaven making massive inroads into state finances, considerable effort went into the designing of the buildings and this shows a typical military establishment of the Kaiser's era. Despite heavy bombing, especially towards the end of the War, a good number of these buildings and their adjacent accommodation blocks survived to stand to this day.

Filling the new naval base in Wilhelmshaven with the necessary official buildings was relatively easy because it was all virgin land and therefore a simple case of dotting houses around the edges of the newly constructed harbour basins. One of the big problems with this development was that many men were not married and came from a long way away. Therefore a substantial backup system had to be created for recreational and domestic purposes. This small and more comfortable 'Seamen's House' was opened in 1903 and continued to be used as a social centre for some time before it was converted into the theatre.

allotment gardens between the Ems-Jade Canal and the dock basin. The site was chosen because it was almost completely cut off from the town and therefore relatively easy to control access to the area without turning it into the usual naval stronghold. The plan was that U-boat crews should live on land while in port and their accommodation should be as homely as possible, so that men could come and go as they wished, without the usual restrictions of a high security area. In addition to this, the base was to provide everything the men needed including comfortable bedrooms, libraries with reading rooms, messes, shops and cinemas, so that they did not need to leave during their free time.

The Ems-Jade Canal was a relic of the early imperial days, large enough to carry fast torpedo boats but not deep enough for cumbersome submarines. The idea was to avoid potent torpedo boats having to brave the hostile waters of the North Sea to get from Emden to Wilhelmshaven. After the Second World War the U-boat base buildings were used as a British boarding school, but almost all have now been demolished and very little of the original remains. Modern Germany is deeply ashamed of its U-boat Arm

Above and below: The Officers' Mess or Casino at Bant (Wilhelmshaven), photographed shortly before it was demolished around the turn of the century. Built in the 1930s, this was Germany's one and only purpose-built U-boat Base until a new one was added in Eckernförde for the Federal Navy. The building on the right, behind the saluting officers, is the furthest most accommodation block seen in the above photo, and the machine house with heating plant and diving tower is just visible towards the left. During the War this also had a small anti-aircraft gun on the top. Those small saplings planted long before the war had grown into massive trees by the time the picture of the Mess was taken, making it impossible to take similar photographs to the wartime shots.

and much evidence of this has been buried together with the rubble from the buildings, without even the slightest acknowledgment of the incredible achievements of those who served in this most important base.

Despite occupying a prominent position by the water's edge, the submarine base at Bant in Wilhelmshaven was hardly bombed and survived the War almost fully intact. Two massive personnel bunkers were built there to accommodate some of the essential offices and U-boat men in port. These men had the strictest of orders to take cover in the air raid shelters when the alarm sounded and only skeleton guard crews were allowed to remain inside U-boats. The main reason for keeping a few men on board was not so much to guard against intruders, but to take any remedial action if the boat was damaged. Bunkers to accommodate submarines were planned but never built.

Of all the naval bases in Germany, Wilhelmshaven is the most rewarding for anyone searching for remains from the Second World War era. Enough scars from long ago are still prominent to make it easy to find locations in old photographs and it is most pleasant to explore the massive harbour. Unfortunately anyone searching for specific names from the past might run into difficulties because a number of them have been changed. Yet, walking around the town one cannot help to stumble upon remains from the Kaiser's era and a number of bunkers are still standing, although some effort has been made to camouflage them. The ground is so wet in Wilhelmshaven that a high proportion of bunkers were built above, rather than below ground, and at least one them has been turned into an interesting museum. In addition to the obvious war remains, there are a number of extremely interesting sites, which appear to be missed by many visitors. Even many specialists coming from as far afield as the United States have not yet found the U-boat Memorial or the other poignant naval memorials in the military cemetery (Ehrenfriedhof) by the town park (Stadtpark). Many walk past the fascinating Garrison Church without absorbing the atmosphere inside created by its unique collection of historic memorabilia.

KIEL (MAIN BALTIC BASE)

Unlike Wilhelmshaven, which was literally drained out of a salt marsh, Kiel seems to have always been there and had almost certainly been frequented for many years by the time the Vikings found it. The name has similar roots to the Scottish 'Kyle', meaning a narrow channel. Along this part of the Baltic there are a number of deep estuary-like indentations in the coast, allowing saltwater to run inland for 15 miles or more, providing natural harbours for any storm. These are known as 'Förde' in German, without an English equivalent; the name differs slightly from the German for a Norwegian 'Fjord', although there are similarities in their natural features. These long stretches of water are certainly no river estuaries, as there is only a little fresh water flowing into them. There is no tide as such in the Baltic and the water level in the Förde is dependent on the wind, which can blow it in or out. However, for most of the time it remains fairly constant. Ice does present occasional problems in cold winters, but for most of the year icebreakers manage

Naval buildings from the Kaiser's era all looked similar, no matter where they stood; the Garrison Church usually formed a central part of the setup. During those years men were expected to attend church parade on Sundays and bigger ships provided their own services on board to prevent the main church from overfilling. Despite some historians making wild claims to the contrary, both the Protestant and Catholic Churches continued to hold a significant grip throughout the Second World War as well. This shows the main naval church in Kiel with the huge administration building from the Kaiser's era towards the right. The dockyard's commanding officer lived next to the church, opposite this imposing office block, close to where one of the main gates was situated.

to keep the main shipping channels open and there was very little disruption even to pre-war ferry traffic to Denmark and Scandinavia.

Kiel Wik, meaning a sandy bay, provided the Imperial German Navy with its main Baltic base; the facilities there were developed so rapidly that they quickly strangled themselves. The town by the naval dockyard and a good number of maritime support businesses grew around the naval base, preventing it from spreading. The Kiel Canal was opened shortly after the beginning of the twentieth century and it was not long before commercial traffic also started crowding the navy out of its own home. The locks for the canal are situated immediately next to the dockyard, cutting it off from Holtenau and Friedrichsort. Finally the First World War defeat put an end to naval development. The huge Imperial Navy Dockyard was closed down by the Allies; it was partly privatised and military activity was restricted to what was called a new Naval Arsenal on the eastern side of the water.

The original reason for developing Kiel as a naval base was that nature had done most of the work in providing a safe anchorage for all weathers. In 1865, when the Prussian

The front of the Kaiser's Naval Administration Block for the Kiel Naval Base, where the commanding officer had his headquarters. The buildings of this period were considerably more elaborate than the plainer, but still fully functional blocks put up during the 1930s.

Baltic Naval Station was moved from Danzig to Kiel, it was possible to accommodate the entire fleet and still leave plenty of room for the majority of military exercises. The larger number of command offices in Kiel, more than in Wilhelmshaven, probably owe their origins to being more accessible than the North Sea Coast. Still today, Wilhelmshaven gives the impression of being beyond the end of the world. The roads of North Germany were in appalling conditions until long after the Second World War and during those difficult years it would have been easier to reach Kiel from the Supreme Naval Command in the capital, Berlin. However, it is wrong to give the impression that the rail connections to Kiel were highly significant. Until recently, Kiel had not been developed as a commercial port and the somewhat limited connections reflected this. Anyone wanting to travel extensively within Germany had to take the local express to Hamburg's main line station and change there for trains to almost all parts of Germany. Today Kiel is a major ferry port and at times it is also overcrowded with cruise ships, but commercial cargo traffic is still limited to handling materials for local consumption, rather than as an import and export centre. Such trade was never won away from the older centres such as Lübeck, Travemünde and until the end of the War Rostock and Stettin also played

Above and left: Wartime accommodation was not only plainer than the earlier elaborate structures, but also fully functional. This bunker could have stood in any of the naval bases and being so low suggests that something heavy was stored inside. The entrance with a huge U-boat badge over the door and trolleys for carrying torpedoes give some clues that this was an important part for submarine operations. Torpedoes were usually supplied without detonators, which came in separate boxes and had to be inserted aboard ships. This ensured that there was no danger of anyone, especially saboteurs, from easily detonating the explosives while they were in storage.

A large ocean-going U-boat in Kiel with a couple of laid-up passenger liners by the piers in the background. These ships provided essential accommodation in the main ports and many naval bases could not have functioned had such floating emergency accommodation not been available.

Training and education formed a vital part of everyday life in the main naval bases and there were a large number of specialist schools. Although some of these were located along the peripheries of operational activities, others were important enough to occupy highly sought after positions in prime locations. This shows the old Naval Officers School, directly on the water's edge in Kiel, before it moved to Mürwik (Flensburg) shortly before the First World War. The building is now used as local government offices.

The 'Marinefachschule' (Technical College) in Kiel. Built in the 1930s, it is a typical example of the functional architecture of that period. Despite being plain with unsophisticated lines, the building is still imposing and practical enough to have served for many years after the War, although the huge eagle with swastika was removed.

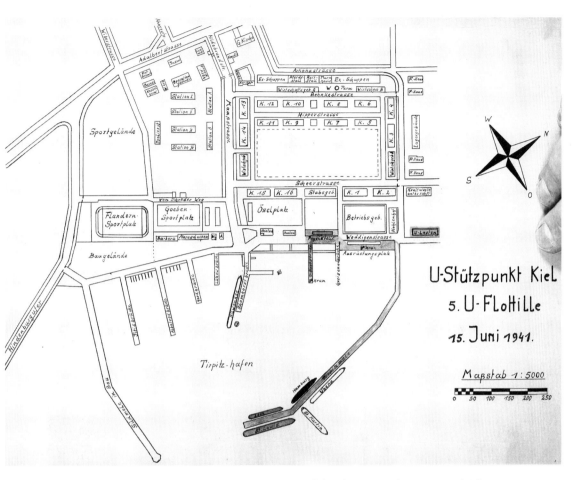

Wartime maps are quite a rarity, so it is most unusual for this one to have survived. This map, showing the layout of the Kiel Naval Base, was necessary because the 5th U-boat Flotilla there specialised in kitting out boats going on their first patrols. So, there were always many new visitors who did not know their way around but still had to find offices, stores, workshops and their land-based quarters.

important roles. The name of Kiel features prominently as a result of being at the Baltic end of the Kaiser Wilhelm or Kiel Canal, but this traffic hardly influenced the town as it rarely stopped for longer than the time it took to prepare a lock for passage.

When the navy set up its first major base in Kiel, the 25,000 people living there occupied the inland end of the Förde around the town hall, still known as the 'Altstadt' (Old Town) and the military moved further out in that large sandy bay at Kiel Wik. The waterfront road connecting the two quickly became home for major offices and villas for the rich started sprouting as well, attracted by the magnificent views across the water. Ship building yards and other supporting engineering concerns grew up on the opposite eastern shore and a number of ferries made it possible for workers to cross the water. The larger shipyards started building their own accommodation for workers and as a result a sizable town grew up in what is now Kiel-Gaarden, Dietrichsdorf and other suburbs.

The three major ship building yards up to the beginning of the Second World War were Deutsche Werke (which should not be confused with Deutsche Werft of Hamburg), Howaldts Werft and Krupp Germania Werft. These had a number of military facilities intermingled with the private concerns. The main naval centre on the eastern bank was and still is the Naval Arsenal, just south of the small River Swentine. The modern Naval Arsenal still occupies this site. During the Third Reich era, there was a naval munitions depot, a victualing depot and an oiling quay. The berthing facilities in Kiel at that time were enormous, with ample deep water in the majority of basins, all with masses of berths. There were at least 58 berths, totalling some 560 metres in length with water deeper than 6 metres, and 62 berths with a total of more than 135 metres with a depth between 3.5 metres and 6 metres. Twenty of the berths had a water depth of more than 9 metres, meaning they could accommodate the biggest battleships of the time. All the quays were equipped with an adequate number of mobile cranes and the harbour also boasted of twenty or more floating dry docks, but these made prominent targets during the War and many were sunk during the last major air raids when the Allied Forces made a final attempt to destroy those installations they had left in relative peace during the preceding years.

Both the Naval Memorial at Laboe, with U995 as technical museum, and the U-boat Memorial at Möltenort are within easy reach of Kiel and remain as reminders of a poignant military past. In addition to these, there are multitude of military remains along the waterfront, but sadly it appears as if their naval past is being slowly eradicated, leaving very few reminders of what happened there during the navy's heyday. A few bunkers, such as the Flandernbunker by the naval base's main entrance, are still standing, but most of these have been so well camouflaged with lush green vegetation that one can pass them without noticing their presence.

The best way of getting around Kiel is by walking along the entire length of the waterfront path from the railway station to the naval dockyard on the western side of the Förde and then taking a ride on a ferry. Two types are available and both provide excellent services for tourists by allowing people to get on and off as required, so that a circular trip can be enjoyed all day long with ample stop offs. The ferries criss-cross the Förde while the harbour tours (Hafenrundfahrt) run around the outside of the water, providing a much better view of the shore.

OTHER NORTH SEA NAVAL BASES

Emden

Emden, Germany's westernmost seaport on the eastern side of the River Ems, lies in an awkward position as far as defence is concerned because the opposite bank belongs to Holland and therefore the navy had no control over what went on so close to the harbour.

In addition to this, reaching the port with ships wasn't the easiest of undertakings. Strong currents, shifting sandbanks and constantly varying water depths put this route a little beyond the fainthearted. Locals, who grew up on the sea had no great problems, but naval officers with clean hands and glowing marks from the naval academy were likely to get stuck. The general situation was slightly different during the First World War, when Emden was used as U-boat base. At that time people got terribly excited when a submarine sailed all the way around the Isle of Wight or managed the entire journey from Wilhelmshaven to Kiel without serious mishaps. One must bear in mind that the first U-boats based in Flanders were taken there by railway, rather than risk the serious problems along the North Sea coast, so in those days it was important to have a base close to an enemy, even if that meant having to deal with awkward obstacles and perhaps objectionable neighbours.

The port of Emden rose to significance after a canal was dug to connect it with the industrial Ruhr. Before that it was most famous for housing an important and rather busy civilian telegraph office with direct connections to Hamburg, Bremerhaven, Bremen and no doubt other cities as well. This centre was in contact with the light ship *Borkumriff* and with the lighthouse on the island of Borkum at a time before radio and telephones became part of the shipping scene. Especially fast, homecoming liners would make contact with Borkum, the first German island after the straights of Dover, so that the telegraph office in Emden could pass on the details and that their time of arrival in port could be calculated. In the days before telephones and inter-continental telegraph lines it was difficult to establish the exact arrival times of long-distance services, which could always be delayed by the weather. This became the first permanent and regular radio connection and therefore it is no wonder that the receiving aerial was higher than the lighthouse. *Borkumriff* had its masts specially extended to hold the wires; it looked something like a knitter's nightmare or a huge spider's web, although the distance between the two was only about 30 kilometres.

The Weser Ports

Bremerhaven on the Weser Estuary can present historians with considerable linguistic problems as it was created by the amalgamation of a number of smaller centres. Collectively these were originally known as Wesermünde and the harbour on the inland side of the main port was known as Geestemünde. This small fishing harbour and was not specifically enlarged until the Kaiser's era, when there was no room for further expansion in the main port of Bremen. Then a number of non-tidal basins with locks were built further out in the estuary. Bremerhaven is now a thriving port with a huge container base and massive vehicle import and export facilities. These have been built on top of some of the earlier features, yet exploring the port is easy and visitors are encouraged to visit. Unlike many British ports, there are good free parking opportunities for watching shipping movements. Although not military, the port boasts an unusually huge steel swing bridge, carrying both a main road and two railway tracks. This tilts and rotates when ships move from one part of the dock basin to another. During the Third Reich's era the port accommodated a considerable fleet of minesweepers to clear both the estuary and river, and there were (and still are) also a number of naval educational establishments.

Cuxhaven

Cuxhaven was originally nothing more than a fishing harbour and served more as a safe haven for boats from Hamburg, rather than as an autonomous port. It was not until the coming of the railways that it developed into an important market and fish processing centre. At the same time it added a major passenger port with a deep-water quay to accommodate the largest liners of the time. Being under Hamburg's administration, rather than Lower Saxony's, meant that much was done to develop an international shipping quay and to support service industries for helping ships move safely along the river. Unfortunately for Cuxhaven, the passenger facilities were hemmed in on a narrow spit of land between two large dock basins, meaning it was difficult to provide much more than a railway station with covered walkway to the quay. Bremerhaven had more space for facilities and by the middle of the nineteenth century it had expanded to relieve Cuxhaven of the majority of its passenger traffic.

During the Second World War, Cuxhaven served as the final stopping off point for a number of ships going further afield. The deep-water quays made it possible for captains and some officers to take the train to Berlin to collect final orders from the Supreme

Old torpedo boats on the left, a modern minesweeper on the right and a group of small motor minesweepers in the middle, berthed in the outer fishing harbour of Cuxhaven. Cuxhaven also had a large, dedicated minesweeping basin on the other side of the huge clock tower. This tower and the long building and are part of a Victorian deep-water passenger quay.

The Minesweepers' 'Kammeradschaftsheim' or Social Club in Cuxhaven. Finding something to do in spare time was a major problem for many naval groups. The men lived in quite harsh and cramped surroundings aboard their ships and needed comfortable outlets for their free-time energies.

Naval Command. Cuxhaven also accommodated minesweepers. These were important for clearing the approaches to the Kiel Canal. After the War, Cuxhaven became a major base for the Allied-controlled German Minesweeping Administration. This was set up with surviving German minesweeper flotillas and remained operational until absorbed by the new Federal German Navy.

After the War the British army of occupation used the country between Cuxhaven and the old naval air base at Nordholz for launching something around a hundred V2 test rockets with their characteristic white and red chequered markings. The launching gear was highly mobile and required nothing more than a stable level platform, so it is almost impossible to find any significant remains. Yet, the Imperial War Museum in London has a fantastic collection of detailed photographs and anyone with a local knowledge can identify some of the buildings in photos showing rockets being pulled to their launching area.

The name Nordholz is hardly known, yet there is a magnificent aeronautical museum on what was originally a naval air ship base from the First World War. In addition to this there was a radio station with radio direction finder to help ships in the North Sea by providing them with their position. These were calculated by using cross bearings from the radio station on Borkum and at List on the island of Sylt. (Borkum was the westernmost radio station and List the furthest to the east and the north.) Sylt was

Above: The small Sanftleben (later Beckmann) Ship Yard in Cuxhaven with the minesweeper M133 on the slip for repairs. This spot in now occupied by a modern office block, but many of the buildings in the background are still there. The café and public house next to it, on the extreme left, are still in business. The building at the end of the dyke, almost hidden behind the main mast, is the all-important meteorological office. The old lighthouse is still standing but no longer functional. It has been replaced with a modern control tower for supervising traffic along the busy River Elbe. The strange objects on the right are buoys in the yard of the Main Buoy and Navigation Aids Depot. Every type of local buoy is stored there to be instantly ready if required to replace a lost or damaged one.

Left: The main building of the former Kiautschou Barracks in Cuxhaven. Troops going out to China were trained here until the beginning of the First World War. The building has been restored and is still standing. As in the main naval bases, elaborate efforts went into the design of these houses to make them attractive as well as functional.

The navy supplied splendid buildings, magnificent ships and its own naval prisons. The cells in the upper part still have their old iron bars over the windows. The size of this establishment, compared to the relatively small naval base, suggests that the prison either catered for other companies further away or there were indeed many unruly men in the navy during the Kaiser's era.

developed as a naval air base and the huge watering or landing site, enclosed by a dyke to maintain a calm surface, can still be seen. Germany never developed suitable aircraft and the significance of this station dwindled once the War started.

OTHER BALTIC PORTS

Flensburg

Flensburg, Germany's most northerly town, was a relatively small trading centre, at one time famous for making rum from imported raw sugar. It always had small ship repair concerns and even slips for building smaller commercial vessels. Getting there from the open Baltic can still be quite a problem. The port lies almost 30 miles inland with a narrow section halfway along the Förde, where it is necessary to make a sharp turn at the same time as hitting this restricted section; the port authorities insisted that any ship bigger than about 500 tons must have a pilot. Although the ship building yard in Flensburg was drawn into the emergency programme to build U-boats during the Second World War, the navy steered well clear of the tricky Förde and never developed a base of any significance there. Yet, Flensburg often features in naval accounts. First, the Naval Officers' School moved out to Mürwik shortly before the First World War, and secondly,

The main entrance of Marineschule Mürwik (Flensburg), the German Naval Officers' Academy since shortly before the First World War, photographed in 2010.

the last German government under Grossadmiral Karl Dönitz was arrested in the sports hall or gymnasium of this school. The third reason for Flensburg featuring in many accounts is that a large number of U-boats were scuttled in the clear waters of Geltinger Bay at the sea end of the Förde towards the end of the War.

Eckernförde

Eckernförde became the headquarters of the Torpedo Inspectorate long before the Second World War because the traffic in Kiel was too heavy for shooting torpedoes from the station's land-based firing system. The water in Eckernförde is also wide enough for ships to sail in at fair speed and turn before heading out to sea again. For this reason the site was chosen for one of the state-controlled measured miles. This facility was open to any ship, often without appointment, and the buoys marking the exact measured miles were supported by a visual sighting system on land, where two markers could be lined up to find the buoys on the water. Today Eckernförde has become a major naval base, with many facilities from Kiel having been moved there.

The Swinemünde Area

The western side of the Baltic was dominated by a number of ancient trading centres, many of which rose to prosperity under the Hanseatic Trading League of long ago. Some of these were big enough to attract a significant naval presence and more were drawn in as emergency wartime measures. However, they did not have strong naval facilities. As one travels further east one comes to a conglomeration of interesting sites. Opposite the town of Stralsund lies Germany's largest island, Rügen, and the tiny island of Dänholm, at one time home of the unit providing initial training for officer candidates. Going further east, one comes to Peenemünde, a small, idyllic village made famous because the German rockets were developed there. This tiny spot in incredible tranquillity was the place from which mankind took the first steps into space exploration. The River Peene runs through a mass of inland water systems, made up of huge lagoons, called Haffs, and connected to each other by canals and natural narrow water channels. The biggest of these is large enough to carry sea-going ships from the coastal port of Swinemünde to

The riding stables of Marineschule Mürwik (Flensburg), where officers have been training since shortly before the First World War. Horses were still a major form of transport in 1939, when this photograph was taken, and many officers were expected to be able to ride, although they seldom had the opportunity to do so.

Stettin, which was Germany's biggest Baltic port and was surpassed in capacity only by Hamburg, Bremen and Bremerhaven.

Heading eastwards by sea along what is now the Polish coast, one comes to the small port of Kolberg, but after that there is no natural or significant manmade safe haven until one reaches Danzig Bay, some 350 kilometres further east. This is not to say that there was no naval presence in the area. There was, for example, a naval radio station at Stolpmünde, but tracing these isolated establishments these days is most difficult and input from local historians is more than necessary. With Swinemünde being the only practical stop off point between the far eastern Baltic and the west, it is perhaps no wonder that the town was developed into a significant naval port and fortified at the same time.

Luckily for history buffs, at the end of the Second World War, the Polish border was moved west from a point about 50 kilometres west of Danzig to about 3 km west of the River Swine. The Russian army of occupation did not show a great deal of interest in the old military relics and the vengeance of the western Allies did not penetrate beyond the borders of their occupation zone. As a result, two fantastic forts from the middle of the nineteenth century remain standing on the banks of the Swine and have now been restored. Details of Fort Aniola, guarding the western shore, can be found on the Internet. Although this fort was built during the age of muskets and gunpowder, it no longer played a significant role by the time of the Second World War and was no longer in a position to seriously protect the interests of Swinemünde.

Due to its significant position and natural facilities, Swinemünde was developed into a major naval base with engineering facilities of all kinds, including the necessary setup for building new ships. Indeed there were three major ship building yards in town and four more 37 miles further inland in the city of Stettin. Stettin was the commercial centre of this area, with significant communications reaching deep into the industrial heartland of Silesia, but it was far away from salt water and the navy preferred to remain closer to the coast. Yet, the navy did make use of the shipyards there and a two Type VIIC U-boats (numbers U821 and U822) were built at the Oder Werke, and U901, also a Type VIIC, at Vulcan in Stettin. In addition to this, several operational U-boat flotillas set up base there towards the end of the War, after invading armies had pushed them out of their earlier homes. The channel between the city and the estuary was shallow and its depth of 9 metres had to be maintained by constant dredging. This meant it could have been blocked too easily in the event of an emergency. The fact that it was compulsory for every ship of any size to take a pilot in order to negotiate this deep-water channel suggests it was not an easy route. The only ships without pilots were a few who frequently used the route and whose officers were especially trained to cope with the arduous conditions.

Swinemünde had excellent quays, capable of holding large ships and a number of well-established dolphin berths for larger warships. There was a permanent minesweeping presence, capable of helping ships going east or west, and a major seaplane base. This, however, never played a significant role because the Kriegsmarine never developed a fleet air arm and many specialist naval pilots ended up becoming U-boat officers. The name of Swinemünde started featuring significantly shortly before the end of the War when the port was used as a dropping off point for refugees from the eastern provinces. They were being evacuated to avoid the horrible tortures being metered out by the advancing Russian armies.

The port also became the last resting place for pocket battleship *Deutschland* (by that time renamed heavy cruiser *Lützow*). The ship supported the army in the eastern Baltic during the first months of 1945 until it was forced out of the Danzig area in April. Heading west, *Lützow* anchored in the Mellin Entrance of the harbour, where it received several hits from the Royal Air Force. As a result the pocket battleship settled on a level bottom in such shallow water that the upper (outside) deck remained above the surface and in such a position that the rear 280-mm gun turret could be used to bombard the advancing Russian army. Most of the anti-aircraft guns and some of the 150-mm secondary armament remained in use as well until the Germans ran out of ammunition.

Stralsund, Sassnitz and Dänholm

Although the town of Stralsund had a naval garrison, it was not a major naval port, but the small island between Stralsund and the island of Rügen played a vital military role during the Second World War period. Men accepted for officer training assembled in front of the main line railways station at Stralsund to be taken to the tiny island of Dänholm for the start of the selection process, and after that their initial training period. They wore their own sport-suitable clothing at the beginning while they were put through their paces to eliminate those who might not cope with the physical demands of the stringent training schedules. Those who remained after the selection process were supplied with naval infantry uniforms until they qualified as officer candidates at the end of an approximately six-week-long period. Only if they passed were they allowed to don on a naval uniform, take their military oath and move on to the Naval Officers' School at Mürwik (Flensburg).

Dänholm was ideal for this sort of activity because it was remote and any military activity there was unlikely to interfere with other local interests. The island had been purchased by the military in 1850, more as a defence base rather than training ground. This was the time when Prussia was at war with Denmark and Wilhelm Bauer built Prussia's first submarine, the *Brandtaucher*. At that time a small harbour was excavated to house a number of small boats, including gunboats powered by oars. So it was indeed on a small scale and somewhat antiquated. The base was abandoned again and later, during the Franco-Prussian War of 1870/71, the island was used to accommodate prisoners of war. This seemed to have worked well because during the First World War it housed prisoners of war once again, this time specialising in officer accommodation. It was not until the early 1920s that both Stralsund and the island of Dänholm were, once again, used as small naval garrison, this time to accommodate a training division. Although the 2nd Schiffsstammdivision der Ostsee (Ship Crew Training Division of the Baltic) moved there in 1922, the facilities were still somewhat antiquated and it was not until 1934-1936 that new accommodation blocks were built. This coincided with the building of a dam to connect the island of Rügen with the mainland and part of this route

Young officers in a practical science lesson. Until the beginning of the Second World War, it was compulsory that all officer candidates had had a grammar school education where classical rather than practical lessons were the order of the day. The majority of youngsters joining technical trades went through a lengthy apprenticeship to compensate and especially officers had to spend long hours on school benches learning the basics to help them through the mechanical aspects which would dominate their career.

cut across a corner of Dänholm. The railway connection was opened first on 5 October 1936 and followed by the opening of the road on 13 May 1937.

Although Dänholm was abandoned at the end of the Second World War, the Volksmarine of the German Democratic Republic used the site until it was dissolved around the unification of Germany in 1989. After that the small enclosed harbour basin became a vibrant home for sailing boats, the military installations were handed back to the city of Stralsund and now there is also an interesting naval museum in one of the old buildings. (Details of which can be found on the Internet.)

Danzig and the Eastern Baltic
The Danzig (Gdansk) area of Germany saw dramatic changes shortly after the end of the First World War. Russia, Germany and the Austro-Hungarian Empire were forced to concede large areas of land to create the new independent state of Poland with a narrow

Dänholm in the Baltic between Stralsund and Rügen Island, where naval officers were first selected before going on to their initial training. The houses surrounding this large exercise area are still standing and can be found on Internet satellite pictures. Each house was named after a ship, with Derfflinger just readable in the distance. These buildings are also good examples of the 1930s architecture with its simple lines.

Although naval officers spent much of their time performing hard physical activities for what is now called team building, they also had to learn how to march and to cope with the highly demanding 'goosestep'. Although this is now often ridiculed, it was incredibly difficult and many troops could not have kept up the rigorous rhythm for any great length of time. This shows officer candidates parading in front of House von der Tann on Dänholm.

The Bay of Danzig as it looks today with a coat of snow. The River Weichsel was diverted long before the war to meet the Baltic to the east of the town, rather than flow straight through the centre.

corridor to the Baltic. Although only about 30 kilometres wide in places, this did cut East Prussia off from the rest of Germany. The victorious Allies also decreed that Danzig, the major city of this area, should be taken away from Germany to become an independent free city. This left the newly formed Poland in a dire predicament of having access to the Baltic coast, but without a significant port. The natural geography of the area did not leave much choice and finally it was decided to develop a tiny fishing village into a major port with the new name of Gdingen. This was a great help to the German Navy throughout the Second World War by supplying a ready-made base with all the facilities anyone could wish for, and on top of that, it was well out of reach of the British Royal Air Force, making it an ideal training centre. From the autumn of 1939 until 1945, it was known as Gotenhafen and then at the end of the War reverted back to its earlier Polish name.

Due to the loss of territories at the end of the First World War the German Navy was left in a dire predicament as far as eastern Baltic bases were concerned. Danzig did not have a significant industrial hinterland and the ship building yards with repair facilities and floating dry docks were supported artificially to bring work into what was becoming a slowly degenerating backwater. The prosperity brought by the Hanseatic League no longer produced profits so the Imperial Naval Dockyard played a vital rejuvenation role in addition to supporting the navy. This was then closed when Danzig became an independent free town.

Gotenhafen (Gdynia), one of Germany's main naval centres, around the beginning of the War.

The main channel in what is probably Pillau. Ice was a major problem, especially in the eastern Baltic where ports often froze solid for several months each winter. This meant ships were locked in or out and training activities had to be curtailed or moved to the North Sea, where inexperienced men could easily find themselves within reach of enemy interruptions.

The only other significant naval base was Pillau (Baltiysk), about 80 kilometres further east across the Bay of Danzig. Long shore drift and persistent westerly winds have created a number of narrow, but impressively long spits of land enclosing vast lagoons behind them. Pillau was situated on the northern peninsula, opposite the end of one such spit. This was most convenient as there were no great commercial docks other than supporting industries for the deep-water ship canal leading to Königsberg (Kaliningrad), the capital of East Prussia. This was not only the main commercial centre, but also had enough port facilities to support the hinterland around it. With the loss of Danzig, the remains of the German Navy moved to Pillau because of its most practical position right on the Baltic coast. As a result a number of headquarters, command centres, offices and other services for the defence of East Prussia were re-established there. Being also well out of reach of the British Air Force, it made an ideal harbour for a variety of training establishments. After the start of the War, Danzig was once again drawn in as a major naval training centre and, in addition to this, it had the necessary facilities to accommodate all manner of ships. Danziger Werft was later used to help with the building of U-boats and was one of only three major shipyards where the revolutionary new electro-boats of Type XXI were assembled.

There were also a number of other small ports that served the U-boat Arm by providing bases for training flotillas, but these were all so small that they are not even mentioned in the secret handbooks produced by the British Naval Intelligence Division. The three most well known of these minor harbours are probably Hela (Hel), Memel (Klaipeda) and Libau (Liepaja), in the far eastern reaches of East Prussia. In fact Libau was no longer German and had been hived off at the end of the First World War to come under the jurisdiction of Lithuania, but German was still widely spoken.

CHAPTER 4
Major Bases that Never Were

Jasmunder Bodden on the Island of Rügen

Towards the end of the nineteenth century, when the Imperial Navy was founded, the new German government was faced with a significant financial problem regarding the creation and development of its naval bases. In addition to requiring one on the Baltic and another on the North Sea, it was also necessary to connect the two with a substantial canal capable of carrying ocean-going ships. The costs of this canal could be partially disguised by promoting it as a commercial rather than military venture; but this massive expense, together with the building of a non-tidal, floating harbour in Wilhelmshaven, made it necessary to choose the cheapest option for the Baltic. So, existing facilities in the natural harbour of Kiel were developed instead of building a proposed brand new port on the island of Rügen.

It must be remembered that the unification of Germany and the foundation of the Imperial Navy came about in 1871 as a result of France having declared war on Prussia the year before. This happened only about twenty years after Denmark had successfully blockaded the Prussian ports. So Kiel, situated about 70 kilometres from Denmark, was thought to have been a good location on which to focus naval activity. Yet Königsberg, the capital of Germany's easternmost province (East Prussia) was some 700 kilometres away. So, ideally Germany needed a base not in Kiel but halfway between the two. The expensive problem was that there were no natural harbours capable of holding large battleships along that part of the coast.

The next problem arising out of the decision to develop Kiel wasn't long in coming. By the outbreak of the First World War in 1914, Kiel had grown so rapidly that the navy was having considerable difficulties in coping with the demands put upon it. The Naval Officers' School had already moved out to Mürwik near Flensburg in 1911, the Torpedo Inspectorate had gone to Eckernförde and several other centres had been farmed out to smaller ports along the eastern Baltic, or they had moved further inland to nearby towns. Kiel was so overcrowded that it was bursting at the seams. There was not even enough space to build a dedicated U-boat base and this was eventually added, albeit after the First World War, in Bant (Wilhelmshaven). That expensive canal between the Baltic and the North Sea remained as a major thorn in the flesh for longer than planned. It had

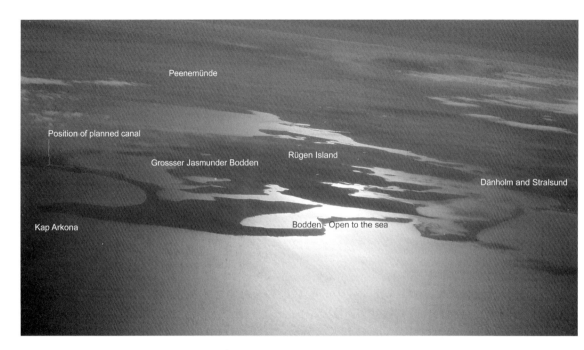

The island of Rügen with Jasmunder Boggen clearly visible. Officer candidates were selected on the tiny island of Dänholm near Stralsund. There were plans to convert the entire Bodden into a major base with huge dockyards as well as the usual berthing facilities.

hardly been completed when new British Dreadnought battleships made it necessary to deepen and to widen it and another set of larger locks had to be added at both ends.

In 1935, when Hitler introduced a new defence law, the naval hierarchy once again examined the earlier proposition of building a brand-new base in what on the north-eastern corner of Rügen Island, now a national park and an area of outstanding natural beauty. Situated only about 2 kilometres off the mainland, this is Germany's largest island, close to what is now the German-Polish border. Poland didn't exist when the Imperial Navy first considered this proposition, and in 1935 the Polish border was almost 300 kilometres further east, putting Rügen conveniently about halfway between east and west. The railway dam, connecting the island with the mainland, was opened in October 1936, making it possible to turn the man-made harbour of Sassnitz into a major ferry port to connect with Scandinavia. So, there were good links between the Reich's capital (Berlin) and this still-isolated part of the coast, making the proposition of a naval base there most attractive. The threat posed by the newly formed Poland provided the impetus to forge ahead with this old imperial idea.

A considerable fortune, probably as much as 10 million Marks, was spent on preparations during the Hitler era, so there are enough remains to mark the beginning of this major development. The first and key step was to find a large, easily defended area of deep water to provide constant access for the biggest warships. By 1938, when the famous Z-Plan was being formulated, this meant the port had to be capable of accommodating ships bigger than the planned *Bismarck* and *Tirpitz*. Ideas for building such big ships were, of course, already buzzing around long before 1935.

The Grosser Jasmunder Bodden, west of Sassnitz, was chosen to form the main part for this new port. Measuring 6 kilometres from east to west and about eight from north to south, it provided the ideal space; this huge bay of enclosed calm water was already connected to the Baltic by a twisting, narrow and shallow water channel. Rather than dredging this complicated route, the navy decided to dig a short deep-water cut to connect the Bodden with the open Baltic. There are hardly any tides in the Baltic, so there were no great problems with varying water levels. This work started around 1938, continued well into the War and was not brought to a halt until the resources for its development could no longer be justified.

Although it has been compared with the British Royal Navy's anchorage at Scapa Flow in the Orkney Islands, Rügen was due to have been far more than a mere parking space for the fleet. The plans included a bustling port with a fully blown naval dockyard, a special U-boat base near Lietzow, to the south of the Bodden (or enclosed bay) and all other necessary facilities, including training centres. All of this would have been protected by massive coastal defence installations. Parts of the new entrance, to the east of the village of Glowe were dredged during the late 1930s and it looks as if the ends of these deep channels are just about visible on Google Maps.

During the 1930s this part of Rügen was incredibly remote and even the isolated and totally man-made ferry port of Sassnitz appeared to be almost cut off from the rest of Germany. Yet, there were good railway connections to the main line network. So, the site was not totally dependent on supplies being brought in by ship and many of the early workers arrived by train. Exactly what happened with these and what they achieved is difficult to ascertain without digging through the fascinating local history. The site was laid to rest during the War, but it wasn't long before post-war authorities took an interest in this development and continued with the project. Much of what has been written is contradictory and it is difficult to separate fact from fiction. On the one hand many accounts describe several forced labour camps in the area and on the other hand the same reports state that workers were eager to work there because the pay was so unusually high. Apparently workers were paid double the average rates. Whatever the case, the naval base on the island of Rügen did not get far beyond the initial exploratory working stage during the Second World War.

HELIGOLAND

Heligoland, an island of less than 2 square kilometres with red sandstone cliffs rising to about 50 metres above the German Bight is strikingly different to the low, sandy continental coast, but even the firmness of this rock couldn't stand up to the ravages of the sea. In 1720 a fierce storm tide washed away many villages along the mainland, totally destroyed the small island of Witt Kliff (White Cliff) near Heligoland and cut the fortress-like island in two by washing away what was then a large area of the Lowland.

The harbour at the landward side of Heligoland was subject to constant bombing attacks but none of these interfered significantly with the U-boat activity as there was a massive shelter to protect small boats. This huge rectangular structure can be seen in the corner of the inner harbour. It is tempting to think that this shows the result of an air raid, but it seems far more likely that the white haze is a cloud rather than smoke, but there are loads of bomb craters on the land.

What remained were the red cliffs and a smaller island of Dünen towards the east. The strange point about these two is that the old Triassic red sandstone and the sandy hills of Dünen, on which the airport is situated, are both resting on younger, Cretaceous chalk; the same rock from which the Downs of England and the White Cliffs of Dover are made. Witt Kliff, which was visible from Heligoland until that ferocious storm of the early eighteenth century, was also made from this same chalk.

This marvellous haven for pirates originally belonged to Denmark. Britain acquired sovereignty as a result of the Battle of Copenhagen, in which Horatio Nelson led the attack, and then in 1880 Imperial Germany swapped its colony of Zanzibar for Heligoland. It has been German ever since. Germany was keen to acquire the island because it is situated about 60 kilometres from Cuxhaven and only about forty-five from the nearest bit of mainland, Eiderstedt, to the north of the Eider Estuary. So, it was strategically well placed for the defence of the German deep-water shipping channels leading to Hamburg, Bremen, Wilhelmshaven and to the Kiel Canal.

That twisting deep-water channel leading to the naval base of Wilhelmshaven, which Royal Navy officers were warned about towards the end of the Second World War (see the section on Wilhelmshaven), is at least some 30 kilometres long and not passable in all weathers. Strong crosswinds made it difficult and often low lying fog obscured buoys marking the channel, making it necessary to close the passage. In winter, ice became an added problem when working the locks to the floating harbour. It was not until the late 1920s that radar installed experimentally aboard the artillery training ship, the light cruiser *Königsberg*, made it possible to get in and out of that treacherous trap in poor visibility. That trap snapped shut fatally at least once during the Second World War, when U31 (Kptlt. Hans Habekost) was sunk in the narrow approach by an aircraft on 11 March 1940 while attempting some diving tests.

So, the Imperial Navy was more than enthusiastic to develop Heligoland as a deep-water naval base, where ships could be kept in instant readiness and not be dependent on the weather or other natural forces to get in and out of port. Heligoland was still a most important base during the First World War, when many of the steam-driven warships could not get much further than the British east coast and temperamental diesel engines in submarines made this a most important stop-off point. The rather significant naval facilities there could, of course, have been easily destroyed by bombardment from enemy warships and, even worse, an invading enemy could prevent German ships from operating in their own home waters. This meant powerful fortifications were necessary. Establishing these was relatively easy because the red sandstone was ideal for hollowing out; a large number of deep tunnels were dug to turn the island into an impregnable fortress.

Thoughts of developing the island into a major naval base had already been considered during the Kaiser's time. The problem was expense and technology; machinery had not progressed far enough to contemplate such an ambitious project. Reasonably efficient mechanical diggers, cement pumps and Hitler's enthusiasm made an impression on Europe at about the same time; this combination rekindled the interest in building a major base along the eastern side of Heligoland. This was not going to be a naval dockyard, but very much like a man-made Scapa Flow, a naval anchorage where warships would be supported by a fleet of supply ships and kept in instant readiness. The major shipyard of Wilhelmshaven, with dry docks and every facility one could wish for, was only a few hours' sailing away, so there was no need for heavy repair equipment. The idea was to provide a safe anchorage; safe from artillery bombardment, submarines, torpedoes and aircraft. The idea was that the island would have more powerful guns than any battleship and there would be several destroyer and motor torpedo boat squadrons to chase even the fastest enemy ship.

The plan was to build two almost parallel, curving walls, shaped something like a huge lobster's claw, at least three times as long as Heligoland to enclose this and the island of Dünen with the airport. In addition to having open anchorage basins, parts of this base were to have moles and floating pontoons at about 45 degrees to the main walls, so that ships could easily get in and out and always have a permanent roadway where they stopped. The large entrance, to the north, was due to have had another wall placed in front of it so that ships had to make a 90-degree turn to enter. The idea was to make it impossible to shoot torpedoes into the anchorage and to make it difficult for uninvited submarines. The place would have been vast, some 3 kilometres wide (from south-west

The western side of Heligoland with the first phase of Project Hummerschere (Lobsters Claw) projecting a long distance beyond the red sandstone cliffs. The wall, running all along the island was originally conceived as protection for the cliffs, but extended at both ends far beyond the island. Had the naval base been built, then the wall would have stretched more than a kilometre or so beyond the imposing stack, known as 'Lange Anna' (Long Anna). The white object a long way beyond the end of the wall happens to be a passing boat.

to north-east) and 6 or more kilometres long (from north-west to south-east). A concrete wall to protect the base of the comparatively soft sandstone cliffs, a set of quays to create a small harbour to the south of the island and a substantial U-boat bunker were all that was ever built.

The majority of the 2,500 inhabitants were not terribly keen on Hitler's new development because large tracts of the highland were placed out of bounds and tourists provided a good proportion of the islanders' income. Fishing, especially for lobsters, no longer produced enough revenue. This building of fortifications was intensified once the War started, although the island never became a significant naval base, despite many guns being manned by men from the Kriegsmarine. Rather than a naval base, it was more a highly specialised fortress with everything such a defensive core required. The biggest guns, with a calibre of 305 mm, could well have dealt a shattering blow against any attacking battleship, and the masses of heavy, medium and light dual-purpose weapons, together with searchlights, sound detectors and radar installations should have coped with any attack, whether it came by sea or air. Yet, the Germans had not counted on the dogged determination of their enemy and had not expected almost 1,000 aircraft to attack at once. This massive raid didn't come until shortly before the end of the War, when the island was finally evacuated because literally nothing remained standing. Once the Allies landed to inspect the damage they had done, they found the underground rooms still so full of ammunition that they used it to blow a huge crater into the southern cliffs, but even this demolition process couldn't destroy all of the underground bunkers; large chunks still exists to draw in tourists searching for evidence of Europe's chaotic times.

CHAPTER 5

Clandestine Centres

The most famous clandestine centre was probably the UAS or Unterseebootabwehrschule (Anti-Submarine School). Although this school had roots going back to the First World War, its covert activities did not start until shortly after Hitler had come to power. On 1 October 1933 Korvkpt. Kurt Slevogt (commander of the First World War's U107 and U71) re-founded the UAS in Barrack Number 3 backing onto Arkonastrasse (Arkona Road) at the Kiel Wik naval base. His brief was to prepare men to man the next generation of U-boats. These had been banned in Germany at the end of the War as a result of the Treaty of Versailles, but clandestine technical development started as early as 1922 to keep abreast with latest mechanical progress; by 1933 it became necessary to conduct trials with a number of boats being built secretly in foreign countries.

Anyone visiting the Anti-Submarine School in Kiel would have been impressed by a highly technical setup dedicated mainly to determining the position of submerged submarines by sound. Since Germany didn't have any submarines, the school acquired a comprehensive collection of records with noises of underwater movements. There were also a couple of old, wooden anti-submarine destroyers from the First World War so that the men could attempt tracking ships at sea and occasionally they had a go with any co-operative foreign submarines that attended some of the naval open weeks.

It was highly unlikely that any visitor would have noticed anything of the undercover side of the establishment. None of these offices had their correct names on the doors and their secret activities were well hidden, even from casual naval personnel who had reason to be in the building on business. The school's staff and their trainees quickly discovered that the other, more interesting department was made up of three sections with Fregkpt. Fürbringer in charge of military training, Korvkpt. Robert Bräutigam dealing with underwater survival and Korvkpt (Ing). Hülsmann responsible for mechanical matters. To do this they built three quite advanced simulators. One of them was an engine test bed complete with electric motors and a clutch connecting the two. There was a set of hydroplane controls set up realistically on a seesaw allowing trainees to get a feel of how boats dived and surfaced, and also a set of main driving controls with an optical torpedo aimer.

The clandestine nature of this school lost its significance in March 1935, when the U-boat Arm was re-founded and the UAS was re-named U-boat School and given the first six new U-boats (U1-U6). Slevogt, who had in the meantime been promoted to

This is rather an interesting picture of Block 4 at the naval base in Kiel. Men had to hand valuables or large amounts of money to the duty officer, whose office was in the room to the right of the door. Such areas were obvious targets for burglars and therefore had reinforced windows and doors as well as safes. Block 3 is the next one along the road and virtually identical to the one in the foreground. Number 3 is also of special interest because it was there where the clandestine Submarine Defence School was established to train future submariners at a time when such activities were still prohibited in Germany.

Fregattenkapitän, remained as the first head of this newly founded institution. Strangely enough it did not come under the jurisdiction of the newly founded submarine flotilla, Flotilla Weddigen, but remained under the control of the Torpedo Inspectorate.

Clandestine technical submarine development started much earlier than the Anti-Submarine School. The first steps for this were taken immediately after the end of the First World War. By that time Germany had not only built the largest submarine fleet but was also near the pinnacle of technical development. This meant that the clause within the Treaty of Versailles to abolish all German U-boats hit a number of leading shipyards especially hard. The building of submarines for export was also forbidden. The War had demonstrated quite clearly that submarines could outperform large surface ships and there were enough underdog nations eager to turn to Germany in order to satisfy their future defence plans. Unfortunately none of shipyards could cash in on the amazing technology they helped to develop; Germaniawerft, Deschimag AG Weser and Vulkanwerft joined forces to create a clandestine submarine development bureau based in Rotterdam (Holland). The initial aim was to keep abreast of technical development and then to use this knowledge for building submarines for foreign powers.

This was not as easy as it sounded at first, although it had been obvious from the outset that none of their combined projects would ever get onto a slipway unless they received more than generous support from rich financial institutions. It was clear from the beginning in 1922 that the development costs were going to be astronomical. The planners had to complete many trials before finding the right solution for some of the new emerging mechanical problems. Yet, despite the drawbacks and deep depression of those times, Ingenieurskantoor voor Scheepsbouw (often abbreviated to IvS) under Kpt.z.S. Walter Lohmann, with two of the leading submarine engineers, Hans Techel and Friedrich Schürer, did manage the almost impossible and created the skeleton for Germany's future submarine fleet from their office in Rotterdam.

This submarine development bureau was moved to Germany in 1932, a few months before Hitler came to power, where it was given the new name of Ingenieursbüro für Wirtschaft und Technik (IGWIT) and more commonly referred to as just Berliner Büro (Berlin Office). It was this later branch from the Rotterdam outfit, which developed the German Type II in Finland, where the staff helped to build the *Vesikko*. The bureau also worked through the initial designs for the new Type VII. This was no mean effort since, among other things, it involved drawing thousands of accurate plans.

Just to complete the picture of submarine bureaus, another one appeared during the summer of 1943, when Ingenieursbüro Glückauf (IBG) was founded to help with the building of the new electro submarines of Types XXI and XXIII. By this time Germany had experienced a number of massive terror raids from the Allied air forces and it was clear that their bombs were not being unloaded against military targets, but aimed at civilian homes with the view of killing and maiming as many people as possible. In view of this, the new development bureau was established away from the major ship building cities and set up in a small town of Blankenburg on the eastern edge of the Harz Mountains. The bureau employed over 1,000 people to prepare something in the region of 18,000 plans for the two new U-boat types. So it made more than a significant contribution to submarine development.

To prevent any confusion, one should mention that another highly successful engineering bureau was added after the War to help with the development of the third generation of submarines. This had the name Ingenieurskontor Lübeck (IKL) and was headed by Ulrich Gabler, who started his career as engineer officer of U564 under Reinhard 'Teddy' Suhren.

Secret Headquarters

The Supreme Naval Command, the equivalent of the British Admiralty, had its headquarters in Berlin at Tirpitzufer next to Landwehr Canal until November 1943 when the building was bombed out and totally gutted. By that time an alternative bunker, codenamed Bismarck, had been completed in Eberswalde, some 30 kilometres north-east of Berlin. Some of the staff moved there while especially essential communication centres remained near the Reich chancellery. The U-boat Chief, Admiral Karl Dönitz, replaced

The remains of the navy's main command bunker Koralle in Bernau, photographed for the German U-boat Museum by Heinz Schüler. This is where the Commander-in-Chief for U-boats had his headquarters after he had been appointed to also become Supreme Commander-in-Chief of the Navy. He therefore needed to keep in constant touch with Hitler's headquarters in Berlin. The U-boat staff evacuated this building only about thirty minutes before the first Russian troops arrived. Apparently the Russians used it for a short while before everything connected to the old German government was demolished.

Grand Admiral Erich Raeder as Supreme Commander-in-Chief of the Navy in January of that year, and another command bunker, codenamed Koralle, in Bernau, also to the north-east of Berlin, was occupied by the U-boat staff. A third command bunker was built near Berlin with the codename Roon, but it was not occupied before the end of the War.

Some essential offices from Bismarck were moved to Varel near Wilhelmshaven shortly before the end of the War. Later some of the staff evacuated briefly to Eutin in Schleswig-Holstein and from there to Glücksburg and Mürwik, both near Flensburg. During this chaotic period what remained of naval operations were also led temporarily from other military centres en-route to these named places. Grand Admiral Karl Dönitz, chief of the navy and, since the end of April 1945, leader of the German government as Hitler's successor, was arrested at the Sports Hall of the Naval Officers' School in Mürwik. Dönitz himself was not with his staff when British troops arrived; he was arrested in the house of the school's commanding officer, the highly successful U-boat commander Wolfgang Lüth. This building now houses the Naval School's outstandingly fantastic Historic Collection and is well worth a visit, despite rather limited opening hours.

CHAPTER 6
Lorient – The First and the Last Biscay Base in France

On 7 July 1940, only two weeks after the French-German armistice, Lorient became the first base to refuel a U-boat in western France. This U-boat was U30 under Fritz-Julius Lemp, who is probably most famous for sinking the liner *Athenia* on the first day of the War. Lorient was also one of the last bases to fall into Allied hands at the end of the War. Its German garrison held out against heavy odds from August 1944 until it was officially handed over to American and French forces on 10 May 1945, some five days after the Instrument of Surrender was signed on the Lüneburger Heath near Hamburg.

The besieged garrison managed to hold out for so long because the Allied forces that headed west from the D-Day beaches stumbled upon unexpected problems. First, American tanks discovered the hard way that the fields of Brittany were similar to those in Cornwall and Devon. The numerous hedges around small enclosures had a core of ancient stonewalls, strong enough to bring a tank to a sudden and exceedingly unpleasant halt if it tried driving through. As a result the swift progress was slowed considerably and bitter fighting with heavy losses on both sides became a feature of this fascinating area. Then, when the troops reached the first major base, Brest, they found themselves confronted with desperate defences. Many of the main centres in this area had been bombed so heavily by Allied air forces that many locals did not look upon the invading army as liberators, but more as devils that had destroyed their homes and livelihoods. This core of unfriendly reception combined with determined German resistance prompted the invading forces to cut off and by-pass Lorient, rather than invade the town.

It took a while for the Allied armies to reach the French Atlantic coast and therefore there had been ample opportunity for the German garrisons there to prepare for battle. Lengths of unwanted railway lines were pulled up and buried deep in the ground to form formidable anti-tank barriers. Naval minesweepers picked up some 18,000 mines from inshore waters, amounting to about half of the defensive minefield and there were enough specialist engineers to convert these for use on land. So, the anti-tank defences were indeed laced with an interesting concoction of death traps for anyone trying to pass over them. A number of coastal guns were also modified, by extending their turning circles so that they could fire inland as well as out to sea. In August 1944, a core of about 6,000 Germans, including a Ukrainian mounted division under the leadership of Major Wiedemann, prepared anxiously for an invasion that never came. This number was considerably less than when the base was still fully operational. Then the artillery detachments alone employed at least 7,000 men and there were probably twice that number in addition to a considerable work force recruited from local people.

The Allied armies didn't take any interest in Lorient at all and didn't even establish a cordon around it. When some experienced German reconnaissance troops prodded the opposition's defences they found only a few obstacles manned mainly by the rapidly growing French Resistance. In addition to preventing anyone from leaving the naval base, it would appear that they also took to firing indiscriminately on Germans and on French farmers. Sadly the French Resistance was also busy humiliating, torturing and executing thousands of so-called collaborators.

Despite the lack of an invasion, life in Lorient was not without serious hardship. The entire area was well within reach of heavy Allied artillery, which also indulged in indiscriminate bombardment, often at the most inconvenient moments, and aircraft continued to drop bombs. Yet, despite this desperate situation, neither the land nor the sea routes were completely cut off and for a considerable time it was possible to acquire important necessities, including live farm animals from St Nazaire. This was the next major naval base, some 100 kilometres further south along the Biscay coast. The German troops locked in these coastal bases were cut off from almost all local information and didn't know exactly where the opposition might have dug in. The situation was extremely fluid, with the invading army constantly on the move; it was therefore impractical to mount a large-scale break out to dash back to Germany. It would have been too easy for poorly defended retreating detachments to run into serious trouble. Therefore the leadership in Lorient took the decision to stay put.

The rapid curtailment of German naval activity in the French Atlantic bases when these could no longer be supplied meant there were several redundant mobile units with enough energy to make their own way back to Germany. Thus anything capable of sailing around the north of Scotland was made ready and a number of essential services were ordered to reach Germany by going cross-country. The Allied air forces had gained superiority over much of the possible routes and at this period in time there was hardly any civilian motorised movement, so any moving vehicles and trains became easy prey for patrolling aircraft. Land routes were not an option for large groups.

Men without transport had to contend themselves with frequent forays into the fields around the town. Locals were even provided with passes so that they could leave and return if they wanted to, but the majority of Germans were not given this freedom of leaving. Military law still prevailed and leaving without permission actually became one of the major headaches for the judicial system. Desertion was by far the worst offence dealt with by the court. It might be interesting to add that the German court within the besieged garrison dealt with some 400 offences committed by Germans, but in all that time only two local French people appeared before the judge.

One of the last evacuations took place on 5 September 1944 when U155 became the last U-boat to leave the bunker. There were no longer any fully qualified submarine commanders in Lorient and Leutnant zur See Ludwig von Friedeburg became the youngest man to command a U-boat. He was born on 21 May 1924, so he was just 26 years old at the time when he finally arrived in Flensburg on 21 October, having sailed around the north of Scotland and called in at Kristiansand on the way. U256 under Korvkpt. Heinrich Lehmann-Willenbrock left Brest on 3 September in an even more dramatic manner. The boat had been so badly damaged that it could not be employed for further action, but despite this, a snorkel was fitted so that the commander of the 9th U-boat Flotilla could evacuate essential items of equipment and important personnel. U256 finally ended her days in Bergen, when she put in there on 17 October after a voyage of more than six weeks.

One could look upon the men of U155 and U256 as adventurers who preferred to challenge the unknown rather than remain incarcerated in a besieged garrison, but there were also another three hundred men in desperate need of evacuation. These were too seriously injured to move under their own power, and the remaining meagre medical facilities could not cope with the severity of their injuries. They would either die or be turned into cripples if they didn't receive urgent medical help. A request to the Supreme Military Command in Berlin for permission to take these men to neutral Spain was turned down and so the hastily converted hospital ship *Rostock* (2,542 GRT) was prepared to attempt the impossible; it left on 19 September 1944 for a breakout through the Atlantic to reach hospitals in Germany. Needless to say, the ship didn't get terribly far. It surrendered to a Sunderland aircraft from the Royal Australian Air Force shortly before being escorted by the destroyer HMS *Urania* to Plymouth.

Although the men remaining in Lorient had to face up to an increasingly mundane life, they had enough resources to form and to train a number of completely new defence units. These were provided not only with ammunition to challenge an attack, but they also expended enough rounds to learn their new trade. About 2,000 of these men had come from damaged ships taken out of commission because the necessary repair facilities no longer existed. There remained also well over 1,000 German specialist shipyard workers, about 1,100 men from the naval artillery and well over 1,000 Luftwaffe ground staff. The vast majority of these had come to the armed services as a result of the War and hardly any of them had been trained for fighting on land. Indeed a very high proportion had hardly handled pistols, rifles or light machine guns. So, this new training was more than essential if the Lorient garrison was going to keep potential invaders at bay.

The astonishing point about Lorient was that many of these men happily accepted the challenge to remain in the garrison rather than surrender unconditionally to become prisoners of war. The Germans knew that surrendering was not an easy option. There were enough stories of men being mown down by machine guns while they were trying to surrender. Lorient was in such an out-of-the-way position that the Germans were in no position to hamper the progress of the invasion force. Therefore they were not put to the test by the Allied demand to 'surrender or die'. Many coastal garrisons found themselves confronted with guns aimed at them from so far away that their own weapons could not have hit them, even if they could determine exactly where they were. So, they really had no alternative other than to give up.

Lorient's biggest problem wasn't shooting, but keeping essential services running and feeding the locked-in garrison. Occasionally it was possible to bring supplies from St

Nazaire along both land and sea routes. Even post continued flowing, although there were gaps of several months between some deliveries. In all there were some fifteen postal exchanges during the 10-month-long siege. During the autumn of 1944 it was even possible to import potatoes from local farms 20-30 kilometres away. The besieged town produced its own butter and cheese from a stock of some 5,000 farm animals, of which about twenty-five were slaughtered each day to provide meat. Although horsemeat featured on French menus, the Germans used such carcasses only for making into soap, another important ingredient needed to keep the people healthy.

The main electricity generating plants managed to keep the essential services going. Workshops in windowless bunkers and hospitals could maintain their daily schedules. There was an immense increase in the numbers needing to see doctors so that outpatient medical services and the capacity of the city hospitals had to be increased threefold to cope with well over 4,000 patients throughout the siege. The essential power supply to these services was maintained because many other places didn't drain too much from the main grid. Small wind and water generators were made from all types of electric motors even if they had been so badly damaged that the wiring had to be taken off, spots reinsulated and the wires rewound.

The only remaining grain mill was badly damaged, but engineers managed to get it going again and later other mill machinery was restored as well. One of these was used for roasting coffee and another for extracting vegetable oils from seeds. Even a distillery was set up to produce alcohol to be used initially as fuel and antiseptic in the hospitals, but it was later produced in such quantities that there was enough to keep the men happy as well. As in many other places at that time, about 5 per cent of the bread flour was finely ground wood pulp, made from flavourless dry timber. Apparently this was hardly noticeable when eating the bread and it helped to fill stomachs. The big problem in Lorient was that timber was a valuable resource as well and hard to come by during the siege. In all, the siege cost the German government about 70 million French Francs, paid to the local population for services rendered. So, this occupation was not a case of a foreign power draining the resources from an occupied country.

Before the War, Lorient was a major fishing centre with a population of about 46,000. It also had a large and important commercial port backed by the necessary supporting heavy industries. In addition to this, it was a major French naval base with large garrison, meaning it had the basic infrastructure required for U-boat operations. This pre-war setup was quickly destroyed by the British air force and much of what the Germans took over from the French was bombed into smouldering ruins by the end of 1943, meaning many of the original inhabitants had either been killed or had left the destruction. Strangely, the Allies didn't show a great deal of interest in the building of the massive bunkers, but once the cement had dried and the fortification were capable of withstanding bombing attacks, Allied air forces appeared in large numbers to punish the French for supporting the German occupation. Much of the town was turned into ruins. Hans-Dieter Brunowsky left a document in the U-boat Museum saying that during the spring of 1943 it took him two days to reach Lorient from Neustadt near Kiel. The train was so full that his group of officer cadets had their heavy trunks sent by another route to arrive later. Once within

Alfred Kroschel, a naval secretary (Schreiber Laufbahn), ended up as warrant officer towards the end of the War. He is an interesting person because he became a prisoner of war twice during the same war. Here he is seen with a young assistant in Brest burning confidential papers to prevent them falling into the hands of the invading army. Some military headquarters had special incinerators for dealing with unwanted papers, but Alfred seems to be using nothing more sophisticated than an old waste paper basket. Shortly after this photograph was taken, he was captured and became a prisoner of war. Not long after this, he was exchanged for American medical orderlies held by the Germans in Lorient. At the end of the War, he found himself for the second time as a prisoner of war. (*Photo: Wolfram Kroschel*)

sight of the coast, the group was surprised to find the train running into such heavy ruins, that it looked like an area of almost total devastation. Yet, despite this, the train halted and the travel organisation worked well. A lorry was waiting to drive the men with their hand luggage through this depressing sea of rubble, out into a warm spring. Going past fields the men found their comfortable new home was a good way from the base, where bombs had not yet fallen. Somehow it was easy to circumnavigate the destruction and the terror which created it.

The end of the besieged Lorient garrison came abruptly during the morning of 7 May 1945, having survived 9 months of being totally cut off from the rest of the world. By that time there was only enough bread left for five more days and meat for two months. Forty per cent of the ammunition remained. The end of the siege was marked during the morning by a dramatic firing of all guns at the same time. Following that they fell silent and awaited the arrival of French and American military representatives. Three days later the Germans surrendered officially. By that time about 1,000 men, including some eighty officers, had been killed and buried in one of two special cemeteries.

The Anatomy of the Naval Batteries to Protect a Single Port

The following information is based on details from Wilhelm Fahrmbacher, the author of apparently the one and only contemporary account of Lorient Naval Base. His book, written during the early 1950s, was based on official documents available at the time and personal memories from men who had served with him in the besieged garrison. This information was recorded while it was still fresh in people's memories, without much influence of hindsight or reference to factual re-evaluation which is frequent in many other accounts. Details of his magnificent book are given in the Bibliography. This information is especially valuable because it comes from one of the few contemporary documents giving an exact location of the batteries.

Coastal Artillery

The coastal artillery was initially made up of the Naval Artillery Detachment 264 (MAA 264) and this also controlled another existing battery on the north coast of the Quiberon Peninsula. Later, another detachment was added as a reinforcement measure. The majority of the guns were quickly placed under concrete, which limited their arc of fire to about 60 degrees over the sea approaches, but shortly after D-Day, preparations were started to modify these arcs of fire so that at least some of the heavy the guns could be trained against attacking land forces.

The following main coastal gun batteries were established to protect the port of Lorient:

Battery Talut	4 x 170-mm guns from the old battleship *Braunschweig* 4 x 75-mm guns were installed later mainly for training. This battery was situated on the north promontory of Ile de Groix to cover the western harbour approaches
Battery Larmor	4 x 75-mm guns later 4 x 145-mm guns, situated on the southern approaches of the port
Battery Kerneval	2 x 105-mm guns from the old cruiser *Berlin* used to guard the narrows approaching the port
Battery Gavres	4 x 75-mm guns later with 4 x 105-mm guns from U-boats
Battery Plouharnel	3 x 340-mm guns of French origin
Battery Seydlitz	2 x 203-mm guns from the cruiser *Seydlitz* on the northern shores of Ile de Groix

Naval Flak Detachments (Marineflakabteilungen)

Naval Flak Detachment 704 (MFA 704) was founded in Neustadt near Kiel in November 1940 and moved to Lorient in January 1941.

Before the move it consisted of:

> 4 batteries, each made up of 4 x 105-mm guns
> 1 battery, made up of medium-calibre AA guns
> 1 battery made up of small-calibre AA guns

After the move it was made up of:

> 4 x 105-mm guns at Locmiquelic
> 4 x 88-mm guns on Gravres
> 4 x 105-mm guns 2 kilometres west of Plouhinec
> 4 x 88-mm guns 1 kilometre west of the Blavetbridge at Bonnehomme
> 4 x 88-mm guns south-west of Kevignac near Locadour
> A searchlight battery with sound detection equipment
> Staff battery near headquarters

One assumes from the printed records that all these guns were dual purpose and could be used against flying and surface targets.

This temporary setup was changed with time and by the summer of 1943 the defences of Lorient looked as follows:

Battery München	4 x 128-mm AA guns just over a kilometre north-west of Port Louis, along the main road to Hennebot
Battery Melsungen	4 x 88-mm guns on Gravres
Battery Mannheim	4 x 105-mm guns east of Locmiquelic
Battery Memel	4 x 105-mm guns near Kerbresel, 2 kilometres south-west of Plouhinec
5th Battery	French 40-mm and 37-mm AA guns in Port Louis
6th Battery	20-mm AA guns east side of the naval shipyard
7th Battery	Searchlight and sound detection gear
8th Battery	Staff battery near Kermoelle Quarters
Battery Pilsen	4 x 105-mm guns near Kernours
Battery Magdeburg	4 x 105-mm double barrelled AA guns, east of Port Louis on main road one kilometre east of Kervern

Naval Flak Detachment 806 (MFA 806) was founded in Wilhelmshaven during November 1940 as part of the Naval Anti-Aircraft Regiment 806 and moved to Lorient in February 1941 with:

> 4 batteries, each made up of 4 x 105-mm guns
> 1 battery with medium-sized calibre guns
> 1 battery with small-calibre guns
> 1 searchlight unit with sound detection gear
> 1 Staff battery

The above-mentioned setup remained but saw considerable modification during the following two months and by May 1941 it was made up of the following:

1st Battery	4 x 105-mm guns on the Larmor–Lomener road shortly before the junction to Ploemeur
2nd Battery	4 x 105-mm guns at Ploemeur–Cosqueric
3rd Battery	4 x 105-mm guns about 500 metres north of Lorient between the west side of the River Scorf and Kerduale
4th Battery	4 x 105-mm guns some 2 kilometres north of the airport by the side of the Lorient to Quimperle road
5th Battery	4 x 105-mm guns at first some 4 kilometres south-east of Pont Scorf, but later moved to Kermabo, south of Guidel
6th Battery	4 x 105-mm guns east of the River Scorf and about 1,500 metres north of Lanester
7th Battery	Searchlight and sound detector in Larmor
8th Battery	Staff battery

This basic pattern was changed and by June 1943 it had taken a more permanent character as follows, with some of the impersonal numbers having been given a German name.

1st Battery Hamburg	4 x 128-mm AA guns east of River Scorf near Manehilec
2nd Battery Hildesheim	4 x 105-mm guns as Battery 2 above
3rd Battery Heidelberg	4 x 105-mm guns as Battery 3 above
4th Battery Halle	4 x 105-mm guns as Battery 4 above
5th Battery	Medium-calibre AA guns west of the port entrance opposite Port Louis
6th Battery	Small-calibre AA guns within the town area to the west of the port
7th Battery	Searchlight and sound detector near Chateau Biviere, 2 kilometres south of Pont Scorf
8th Battery	Staff battery

Naval Flak Detachment 807 (MFA 807) was founded in February 1941 in Cuxhaven and moved shortly afterwards to Lorient where it was set up on a temporary basis until the summer of 1941. A number of the guns were first tested at sites already occupied by other artillery sections. At this stage the Detachment had 4 x 105-mm guns and 8 x 88-mm guns plus a variety of smaller calibre weapons and a searchlight with sound detector, but it seems highly likely that more weapons were acquired after the arrival in France. Exactly what was available seems to be uncertain but it appears highly likely that the following sites were occupied from the beginning of 1942 in addition to those already mentioned.

Battery Christoph	Medium and small-calibre AA guns by the Christoph Bridge in the north of the town
Battery Werft	Medium and small-calibre flak in the shipyard arsenal east of the River Scorf
Battery Town	Small-calibre flak at Place Bisson and a further gun(s) at the airport
Battery Hafen	Medium and small-calibre flak south of the town and to the west of the port
Battery Einfahrt	(Einfahrt means entrance, not one journey) Medium and small-calibre Flak to the west of the bay approaches at Kerneval
Battery Ost	Medium and small-calibre Flak to the east of the bay approaches in the Citadel at Port Louis
Staff Battery	2 mobile light flak units on Ile de Groix 1 mobile light flak unit temporarily on Iles des Moutons by Corcarneau 1 or 2 light flak units of the Quiberon Peninsula 1 mobile flak unit on an island in Pointe du Raz (Raz de Sein) to the west of Audierne

The above-mentioned setup remained operational for about 18 months before all of the sections in the Lorient were reorganised. Following that, Naval Flak Detachment 807 was made up of:

Battery Pellworm	4 x 105-mm double-barrelled guns east of Lanester and north of the road leading to the Bonnehomme Bridge
Battery Plauen	4 x 105-mm guns north-east of Lorient near Locadour
Battery Posen	4 x 88-mm guns 1 kilometre west of Bonnehomme Bridge, later moved to the dock area
5th Battery	Medium and small-calibre flak in Lanester
6th Battery	Medium-calibre flak mobile unit started from Concarneau and eventually reached Lorient by train
7th Battery	Searchlight and sound detector in Toulhoet on the eastern edge of the town between Scorf and Blavet rivers
8th Battery	Staff battery
Battery Magdeburg	1 kilometre east of Kernern. Was later also in the centre of the town and after that it was moved to Lanester

Naval Flak Detachment 708 (MFA 708) was established in Kiel during April 1942 with men from the Naval Flak Regiment. It was moved to Lorient and became operational there during May 1942.

1st Battery	4 x 105-mm guns on Ile de Groix later moved to the mainland
2nd Battery	4 x 88-mm guns on Belle Ile
3rd Battery	4 x 88-mm guns on Belle Ile
4th Battery	4 x 105-mm guns Lorient and Granville
5th Battery	12 medium and small-calibre guns on Belle Ile and Ile de Groix
6th Battery	12 medium and small calibre guns on Belle Ile and Ile de Groix
7th Battery	12 searchlights of 2 metres in diameter and 12 medium and small-calibre guns on Belle Ile and Ile de Groix
8th Battery	Staff battery on Belle Ile
?	4 x 75-mm flak gun of a Luftwaffe type originally on Belle Ile later moved to a variety of other locations

Naval Flak Detachment 817 (MFA 817) was founded during May 1943 with:

Battery Rostock	4 x 105-mm double-barrelled flak guns situated between Kerneval and Larmor
Battery Pellworm	4 x 105-mm double-barrelled flak guns east of Lanester and north of the road to Bonnehomme Bridge
Battery Magdeburg	4 x 105-mm double-barrelled flak guns about 1 kilometre east of Kervern
Battery Hannover	4 x 105-mm double-barrelled flak guns 1 kilometre west of Lanveur

This was modified during the autumn of 1943 as follows:

Battery Rostock	as above.
2nd Battery Remscheid	4 x 105-mm double-barrelled flak guns on the road from Larmor to Loemer, about 300 metres from the junction to Ploemeur
3rd Battery Rossitten	4 x 105-mm guns at Ploemeur – Cosqueric
4th Battery Rossleben	4 x 105 mm guns at Kermabo south of Guidel
5th Battery	6 x 40-mm and 6 x 37-mm guns first on Belle Ile, then Quiberon. Suffered considerable losses during an infantry action. Reformed in Kervaugen, 1 kilometre west of Kerneval
6th Battery	12 x 20-mm flak in Quilisoy on the south bank of the River Ter, almost exactly opposite the U-boat bunkers
7th Battery	12 searchlights probably around Marmor
8th Battery	Staff battery
9th Battery	4 x 128-mm flak guns about 500 metres south of Kerloudan

The flak detachments mentioned above were, of course, drastically changed once the garrison was cut off after the D-Day landings.

Without going into details of individual guns installed in coastal batteries, the following might be interesting.

- 105-mm Flak differed considerably from the same calibre deck gun fitted to U-boats and smaller surface ships. These deck guns could be trained high to aim at aircraft, but this was so awkward that it was hardly done. In any case, the deck guns fired single cartridges loaded manually, without any form of even semi-automatic loading system. The Flak version of the 105-mm gun could be depressed for use against surface targets and had a range of a little more than 15 kilometres.
- 88-mm Flak as above, but with a slightly shorter range.
- 20-mm Flak was available in a variety of different types, as single barrelled, double barrelled and quadruple versions, with some of them under licence from Oerlikon in Switzerland.

The majority of these guns were transported from Germany without their steel shields, leaving many of the Lorient batteries somewhat exposed. Some detachments had enough transport to bring their own searchlights from Germany. These generally had a diameter of 1.5 or 2 metres, except the 20-mm guns, which were often supplied with 600-mm diameter lamps.

On arrival in Lorient, guns were placed on firm foundations or in places where a firm base was already available and surrounded by an earthen mound. In many cases this was intended to hide the gun and to protect the crew from the natural elements rather than as a shield against attacks. At the end of 1941 the Todt Organisation started building more substantial accommodation for both anti-aircraft and coastal artillery batteries. However, for some reason Lorient was not placed high in the order of priorities and many of these were never completed. The initial plans were to first place both the batteries and their command centres under concrete and then add bunkered accommodation and living quarters as well, but this latter phase was hardly completed in Lorient.

Radar started playing an ever-increasing role as the War progressed; sadly many history books give a slightly wrong impression of the effectiveness of German radar. Germany developed a most efficient radar system some years before it was brought into use in Britain, but it was intended as a radio range finder to be switched on after targets had been sighted visually. The reason for this was that radar impulses travelled over considerably longer distances than those from which the sender could register an echo. Therefore they could easily give away the location of small German ships to superior enemy forces, without the operator knowing what was going on around him. Shortly before the beginning of the War, the German government lost interest in this new invention and the principle was not fully developed. However, by the end of 1942 there were a number of reasonably effective radar sets being used by permanent shore stations. The most common of the early types, the Würzburg Riese Radar, had an effective range

Right: It is quite obvious that this is a soldiers' home in Lorient. Although Germany requisitioned whatever was needed in occupied countries, finding the right accommodation was not easy and often considerable effort went into making factories, cinemas, schools or other large buildings comfortable. This went as far as providing suitable furniture and having pot plants and flowers in the right places.

Below: Officers' accommodation in Lorient. As many German bases were built along picturesque coasts, there was no shortage of hotels for providing accommodation. Some of these looked plain from the outside, but they provided a high standard on the inside and many were famous for their good quality food.

of about 40 kilometres. The new fast Mosquito aircraft had a top speed of 318 mph (about 511 km/h) so this equipment gave a warning of at least 5 minutes and often much more, which was enough for trained gun crews to get ready for action. The duty team would have been sleeping close to their battery while standing down. The performance of the radar equipment was considerably improved and by the middle of 1943 it was possible to more than double the effective range. Under good conditions the radar could detect aircraft at a range of well over 100 kilometres. Many of them were set up close to existing searchlight batteries, so that the radar crews could make use of the existing domestic facilities.

Getting the anti-aircraft defences going took some while and at first the naval batteries came under jurisdiction of the Luftwaffe, but by the summer of 1941 things had progressed sufficiently for the navy to command and supply both the coastal artillery and the anti-aircraft batteries around their bases.

Attacks against Lorient started more as a nuisance rather than a serious threat and it was October 1942 before the Royal Air Force appeared in strength with both high explosives and incendiaries. These massed attacks were interlaced by either single or small groups of aircraft dropping mines in the harbour approaches, but these planes were often spotted, even if the position of the mines could not be made out. The channels were then swept clear before valuable shipping was allowed to pass. This had an irritating delaying effect without causing serious damage or loss of shipping. The first serious big air attack came on 21 October 1942 and was followed by several more devastating bombing raids, sometimes as many as one per day for a period of about a week.

The civilian population suffered enormously and many crews of small-calibre anti-aircraft guns in the built-up areas were put out of action with a high loss of life, but the damage and the disruption was repaired again so quickly that the output of the U-boat base was hardly effected. This, together with a good number of aircraft being shot down, helped to maintain morale, despite some serious communication problems. The biggest of these was due to the Todt Organisation having carefully buried telephone and telex wires. This now proved to have been a great disadvantage because small bombs often cut the lines and it was virtually impossible to find the location of the break. A few weeks before Christmas 1942 the Royal Air Force changed tactics and showered the target area with phosphorous and with bombs which produced a shower of highly volatile oily liquid. Both were exceedingly unpleasant and much more frightening that the high explosives intermingled with incendiary sticks. Civilians were terrified and the morale of soldiers was also deeply undermined.

The German High Command responded by sending heavier anti-aircraft batteries to the base and also establishing a chain of fog making plants. This system came with its own fog-making crews, but it never worked terribly well along the French Atlantic coast. Other than St Nazaire, there were not enough fog generators to effectively smother the huge area of the naval base. In Lorient there were too many rivers with well-defined landmarks to make the sighting of the main targets especially difficult. This was made worse by an adverse Atlantic breeze interfering with the artificial clouds. Despite anti-aircraft batteries hitting a good number of their targets, the air attacks continued with increasing ferocity, causing considerable loss of life, destroying many French homes and causing serious disruption, but none of them ever stopped or seriously delayed any U-boat operations.

Lorient was originally established as a German naval base to house the 2nd U-boat Flotilla and later also the 10th as well. It had facilities for dealing with small and medium submarines but most of its bunker space was designed to cope with the long-range, ocean-going boats of Type IX. Other than this, there were hardly any other boats under the jurisdiction of the Fleet or the U-boat Commands. Other vessels in port belonged to either the Security Forces (Sicherheitsverbände) or shore-based establishments. These consisted mainly of traditional minesweepers, submarine chasers and a variety of patrol boats. In addition to this there were a few ships from Germany's speciality unit, Sperrbrecher or mine detonators. These were merchant ships surplus to requirements and filled with ballast so that they floated fairly deep in the water, but would not sink easily when hitting a mine. They were filled with a variety of floatation aids, often nothing more than empty boxes or empty tins, but peat was also used. The crew was provided with special accommodation so that they could cope with detonating mines. The plan was to sail in front of valuable ships to explode mines in their path.

The vast majority of these security vessels were converted fishing boats rather than purpose-built varieties from Germany, and each one would have needed a crew of 25-50 men and the smaller boats 10-20 men. The 2nd Minesweeper Flotilla undertook the main

Although it is not clear where this picture was taken, it shows the type of vehicles 'homemade' in Lorient after the naval base was cut off from the rest of the country. Guns were mounted on all manner of heavy vehicles so that they could be moved quickly to repel and attack from any quarter.

Left: It looks as if this car has been especially rigged with U-boat success pennants for some higher officer who is either on the way to receive an important medal or leaving the base to move to another post. A large number of cars from the central car pool were allocated to specific officers and had to be ready at any time for when they were required. The initials (WM meaning Wehrmacht Marine – Armed Forces Navy) on the number plate indicate that this is an official naval car.

Below: Depending on the area, in some bases cars without drivers were made available from the central car pool for sea-going officers with driving licences to be used for pleasure while they were in port. In some places traffic was so chaotic that cars came with professional drivers, who knew their way around foreign roads.

minesweeping activities with its modern M35 boats. These had a crew of just over 100, with what was considered permanent quarters aboard the ships. Their oil burning engines could manage a top speed of 18 knots and allow them to cruise comfortably at 10-12 knots. This made it possible for some of them to be called back to Germany shortly after D-Day. Many earlier oil-burning boats were converted to run on coal due to wartime shortages and these had neither the speed nor the endurance to attempt runs back to home waters. Although some of these deep-sea trawlers could remain at sea for several weeks, the majority were too small to be out for more than a few days at a time.

Getting these ships to the west of France during the disarray created around the Dunkirk evacuation was considerably easier than moving ships back towards the end of the War.

The majority of small auxiliaries were supposed to have been there to either keep unwanted guests out, but more often they were employed for helping invited ones in and out of port. The combined firepower from U-boats and escorts was initially sufficient to prevent serious mishaps in the treacherous harbour approaches. During the U-boat's heyday there were over twenty tugs and some forty supply vessels of all types to service ships in the harbour and to carry provisions to bigger units. There were also about twenty-five small patrol boats for moving all manner of small cargoes and men around. The naval dockyard also had six floating cranes in addition to many land-based cranes on the quaysides. Although there was a reasonable rail network, many of the buildings occupied by naval command centres could be reached only by road. A pool of something approaching 400 vehicles was kept operational by a special unit, which also supplied many of the drivers. This vehicle pool contained cars, lorries, buses and some motorbikes. In addition to this, some of the higher commanders had their own command cars and some even had aircraft placed at their disposal.

CHAPTER 7

Joining the Naval Command Centre in Boulogne

Travelling during wartime with a large military unit may have been easier, even if it was considerably more uncomfortable than moving around in small groups or on one's own. Post-war propaganda has been so efficient that many people believe only German undesirables were always transported in cattle trucks, but this was not so. Large numbers of German soldiers were also moved in goods wagons. These were not comfortable at any time of the year and terribly hot in summer. During excruciatingly cold winter days each wagon was supplied with a stove and a pile of coal. Not ideal, but it did move large groups of men over considerable distances. The War put an enormous strain on communication networks and the German leadership considered it important to interfere as little as possible with the existing infrastructure. In view of this, military trains were often slotted at short notice into complicated local networks, which could result in infuriatingly slow progress. When looking at the question of transporting people in enclosed goods wagons, one should also bear in mind that many German civilians travelled in empty, open top coal trucks. These were often dirty and so crowded that there was only standing room with not enough space to sit, even on journeys lasting several hours.

The following account based on Volkmar König's logbook is of special interest because he not only describes how he and a few colleagues reached the French town of Boulogne during the height of the War by using regular train services, but he also provides an impression of what life was like in a newly seized foreign naval base preparing for what people still think was a planned invasion of the United Kingdom. Yet today we know that the massive troop movements along the Channel coast were to encourage Britain to join one of several peace proposals and Hitler did not have a consolidated plan for crossing the English Channel.

It was Saturday, 24 August 1940, two months after the German-French armistice, that Volkmar was woken from his lunchtime catnap with instructions to report immediately to his commanding officer at the Naval Officers' School in Mürwik, where he was still a cadet in training. He and a number of other cadets were handed written postings to a land-based naval unit in Boulogne (France). This instantly increased the pace of life; cases had to be packed, unwanted items were sent home, heavy luggage had to be addressed with the new military post number and handed in at the transport office. It was already

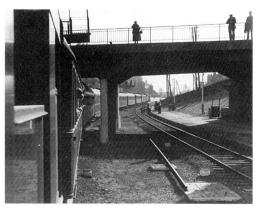

Left and above:: All the armed forces ran special trains between their foreign bases and Germany and these were often so over-subscribed that heavy luggage had to be transported by lorry on journeys lasting several days. Even regular military trains were slotted into existing schedules and it was not uncommon for them to wait for long hours because other operational forces had to be given priority. So waiting in sidings was a common feature. Yet, all this was quite well organised and the navy provided its own mobile catering service for such trains.

late by the time these preparations had been completed and then everybody had to be ready for waking at 3.45 am the following morning in order to catch a six o'clock train from Flensburg to Hamburg. None of the cadets were given any ration cards; therefore they could buy only the simplest of meals in Hamburg, despite having to wait there until half past four for their connection to Bremen and beyond.

Volkmar managed to make a long-distance telephone call to alert his family that he was passing through his hometown. Such calls were not easy and made it necessary to first contact an operator at the telephone exchange who would then hopefully make the necessary connection. Of course the phone call was worth it, mum supplied a generous portion of packed foods and also a good volume of sweets. Yet the meeting was brief and it was not long before the cadets resigned themselves to sampling the sweets while reading cheap novels from magazine-type books as their train lumbered westwards.

It was midnight by the time the train pulled into an almost empty station in Cologne and some of the small group found an empty room at the posh Astoria Hotel close to the station. This would normally have been a little beyond their pocket, but they were travelling on state business and the navy was paying the bill. Volkmar felt very much at home there because the wallpaper in the room he shared with two others was the same

In addition to carrying men, military trains also transported vital war supplies and this shows one of the navy's torpedo transporters disguised as a beer wagon.

as he had at home, but there wasn't enough time to enjoy the serenity. They were awake again less than six hours later to catch the next train to what they thought was going to be Paris, but the carriages were from the Dutch railways and the first foreign stop was indeed in Holland, not Belgium or France. Pulling into a station the men were surprised to see a multitude of traders on the platform selling cheese, honey cake, alcohol, chocolate and a vast variety of fruit, all at exceedingly cheap prices. They were also impressed by a large number of canals with almost every bridge across them demolished. Vital bridges had been temporarily rebuilt since the fighting of a couple of months ago and there were a number of shot-up bunkers, but otherwise no signs of any war. What may be strange to modern readers is that at that time none of the men considered themselves to have been part of the Second World War. Volkmar described seeing 'mortars from the World War' left standing as a monument in one of the stations.

The journey included a planned 50-minute stop in Brussels where the men had the opportunity of taking a brisk walk through the city. This was most amazing for the cadets. They met a vast multitude of girls with incredibly heavy makeup and virtually everything was available without ration cards at prices the youngsters could afford. Volkmar had enough time to buy a shirt before returning to the train for their next overnight stop in Lille. There was only a limited amount of war damage, but the young men did meet a goods train packed with refugees – described by Volkmar as a heap of monstrous misery. Apparently the people, with the meagrest of belongings, had been on the move for three months back and forth without finding refuge. Yet despite this most depressing and heart-breaking experience, the men found everything for their journey was well organised. There were plenty of bars with many German soldiers. The cadets noticed that almost every officer was accompanied by a pretty French girl, all with the wildest of makeup. Accommodation may have been basic, but breakfast was plentiful and they had a lot of time before catching the next train to Calais at around midday.

The cadets noticed a most dramatic change after leaving Lille. There was still hardly any war damage but they saw masses of shot-up cars along the roads and almost every

A large number of lorries joined convoys for regular journeys between far-off bases and Germany. This provides a good impression of a large lorry of the period and one can see that they were not much bigger than a modern 4x4. The huge lorries, dominating our modern roads, did not appear until many years after the War. One has to bear in mind that motorways hardly existed and many of the main roads were nothing more than single or narrow double-track country lanes, often with the most appalling surfaces to make such journeys long and uncomfortable. Such comparatively slow-moving groups along lonely roads were more liable to be attacked than faster trains. Therefore different routes had to be thought out to prevent the opposition from planning ambushes.

station they passed had been destroyed. The part of Calais where they ended up was nothing more than a heap of ruins with a nauseating smell of rotting bodies hanging in the sultry air. The windows of their accommodation had been blown out and boarded up with timber, making the interior dingy and not terribly pleasant. There was no option other than to wait for another train which was due to leave the following day, despite their destination, Boulogne, being only a few miles further along the line. Not wanting to put up with the horrid smell and the mess, the group made for the beach through what they described as a filthy town without any decent bars. They even found the wreck of a man from the Todt Organisation lying in the filth and made a point of escorting him to his lodgings. French wine was cheap, but it contained enough punch to hit the unwary hard. The walk was more than incredible. The men didn't find any human bodies but there was a burnt out stable with dead horses still in their boxes. The young men found hand grenades lying around, guns, ammunition, clothing, tin helmets. Enough to fit out an entire army, if one wasn't too finicky about the condition. The fact that the War

There were plenty of small bars in the occupied countries happy to serve German soldiers during the wartime occupation; many sailors preferred the local flavour with some female influence rather than the rigidity of the naval recreation centres.

was still in progress was brought home later that evening, after the group had settled into their temporary accommodation. The darkness was suddenly illuminated by the flickering shadows caused by searchlights and then anti-aircraft guns woke those who had already gone to sleep. The incredible hammering with their loud stuttering staccato lasted for only a short time while a few aircraft flew overhead, heading inland. Suddenly the lights were shut down and the noise ceased again, leaving everybody for a hot but peaceful night.

The following day another train took the men along the coast from where visibility was good enough to get their first view of England's south coast, but they were more impressed by the size of the fortifications and the guns being installed along the route. Boulogne hit the group with exceptional ferocity. Volkmar described it as a filthy nest with many children wearing nothing but rags. There was nothing to buy and it looked very much as if civilisation had passed the place by. Everything was dilapidated, leaving the newcomers a little shocked by the world they had been sent to. Nobody seemed to know exactly what to do with the newly arrived cadets and at first they were shunted from one job to another, working longer hours than the lowest class of labourers without much of a clue of what they were really supposed to be doing. It was not until later that a captain from the reserve detailed each one of them to their new posts, but even this new division of labour didn't last long before they were told to remain as a group and to await new orders.

Volkmar looked upon his superiors as a group of casual reservists who were definitely not sharp enough for winning a war. The serenity they had got used to evaporated later

A group of civilians moving house while being watched over by a German guard. This barrow was quite sophisticated as it had soft rubber wheels. The majority had cart-like wooden wheels with iron rims. Carts like this could be hired and were used by both civilians and the military for moving all manner of heavy goods.

when large 38-mm guns opened fire against the English coast, aircraft roared overhead into the Channel and it seemed as if their world was dropping from one pandemonium into another without anyone doing anything positive to win the War. One of the big problems was that this hellhole was occupied by only a few Germans from the so-called spearhead, and another 6,000 or so were expected to arrive later to man the massive guns being established along the coast. This meant that the ruins had to be converted into habitable accommodation, but finding such emergency quarters was not easy and getting what there was ready for occupation was just as difficult. A compound occupied by British forces had been evacuated so quickly that many private possessions were left lying around; the men devoted some time to reading love letters. Everything was appallingly dirty, making the men wonder how people actually had lived in such filthy surroundings.

The work in hand varied from something as simple as demolishing bunks in ruins and erecting them elsewhere, to working out the exact times of the local tides. The French may have had their own tide tables, but these were thought to be too unreliable for the boats being used by the Boulogne Port Protection Flotilla and more accurate information had to be calculated. This tedious task demanded more brains than the average youngster from ordinary school could muster, and the arithmetic of older officers had become too rusty. So the cadets with their fresh grammar school mathematics were called upon to do the job. This rather exacting task also involved taking measurements to find out exactly how much water there was in the harbour. Again the military considered local information to be too unreliable and needed their own exact measurements for when German ships might want to take refuge in the port. The food provided by the German military was pretty appalling and much inferior to what the cadets were used to back home, but it didn't take them long to find tastier local sources and stocks of good quality cakes were not long in coming. These quickly started to form an important part of the cadets' diet and there appeared to be no shortage in their supply. The French who remained in town were most obliging.

Both the Germans and the French prided themselves in their production of excellent cakes; after the start of the War, there were a number of well-qualified cake makers among the called-up recruits. So, the tradition of afternoon coffee with cream cakes continued as a feature as long as the ingredients were available. The shoulder straps of the man on the left indicate that he is a warrant officer.

Once down in the harbour Volkmar came across a fellow cadet from Mürwik who had been posted a few weeks earlier and now commanded a small fishing boat. The boat had been converted for patrolling far out at sea and often headed as far as the Kent coast. These undertaking were no pleasure cruises and a number of the crew were wearing naval uniforms with Luftwaffe accoutrements, given to them by appreciative airmen who they had fished out of the water. There was certainly a great demand for all types of fast boats for collecting crashed airmen and many of these craft often returned with a good number of thankful airmen on board, so it was gratifying work.

It didn't take too long before everybody realised what was afoot. The German Navy was making preparations for the invasion of England and plans had to be drawn up for accommodating a large number of river barges. These had been modified so that they could be unloaded over the bows on a beach and they had their bottoms strengthened by adding a layer of concrete. This was also supposed to make them more stable in the rougher seas. It appeared as if everything that floated was being assembled in Boulogne, no matter what condition it was in. These barges came from all over Germany, although Volkmar didn't know at the time that the men collecting them were ordered to take only vessel surplus to requirements and many of them were no longer good enough to carry cargoes along the large river and canal systems.

Long after the War, the author interviewed a number of men driving such huge motorised barge monsters along the inland waterway system, to ask how such craft would fare when crossing the Channel. To appreciate their answers one needs a good understanding of rude German words, all adding up to such a question being more than ridiculous. River barges could only have crossed the sea on the calmest of days. So, what Volkmar is describing is one of the biggest deceptions of the War, but this fitted so well into the British propaganda system, that an invasion of England is still believed by many to have been Hitler's goal, despite there being hardly any serious evidence of this in contemporary records.

The men manning this incredible armada were civilians who may have once read a book about the sea, and a few might have been able to row a small boat hired for use on a pond in a local park, but they had no clue about how to get the amazing fleet across what is one of the most unpredictable waters, with strange currents carrying the unwary often in the opposite direction to where they need to go. To make matters even worse none of the officers had any idea about how to manage the vessels they had been allocated and practise was obviously going to be a major part of these preparations. It all seemed stupid and many wondered what was going on. It felt like having been more like an ants' heap, with everybody busy but not achieving a great deal towards a sensible combined objective. Things got even worse when more troops arrived, most of them from the army with a dreaded fear of the water, but still having to practise a variety of wet activities in the harbour. British air force planes appeared regularly, but often gave the impression that they were more interested in watching the chaotic exercises rather than interfering with them. Bombs were dropped occasionally but it took a while before men made voluntary use of the air raid shelters. The transports in the harbour seemed incapable of crossing the sea and their crews incapable of steering them very far. It all seemed to be a rather pointless and chaotic exercise rather than a serious attempt. Many of the naval officers took to concentrating on the better aspects of the French cuisine rather than trying to sort out the mess. Volkmar and his fellow cadets washed in the Naval Command Centre, but the men outside were considerably worse off. There were only half a dozen slow-running taps for more than several hundred men, meaning the recently converted civilians in their new uniforms had to make do without washing. At least the nauseating smell of rotting flesh continued to dominate the air when the wind was in the right direction, so the excess body odour didn't worry the sailors too much.

CHAPTER 8

Problems with Southern Europe

THE U-BOAT BASE AT SALAMIS, GREECE

The following is based mainly on an account by Kurt Sommer, an Obermaschinenmaat (Chief Petty Officer Mechanic) with the 23rd and 29th U-boat Flotillas, and on documents from Otto Wagner, a Petty Officer in the Administration section of the Salamis U-boat Flotilla.

The move to the Mediterranean started as a mysterious activity for a variety of people being assembled in Neustadt near Kiel. At first it looked as if a new U-boat crew was being woven together, but then, when administrators and a cabinet maker were added, the men guessed that this assumption could be wrong; the growing group would probably not commission a new ship. Later, when they were supplied with clothing for land-based troops, they were fairly certain that they were not going to sea, but some of the men still believed this was some type of cover. All of them had arrived in naval uniforms and they all had at least a little experience in U-boats. U-boat men were in short supply and why assemble such a team of specialists for anything else other manning a U-boat? Things became even more curious when the men discovered that their leader was not a commissioned officer but a chief mechanic with a warrant officer rank. Nothing seemed to fit together and the only definite clue came from idle chat with colleagues in the administration section who told them they were assembling teams for going to the Balkans. The German word for Baltic is Ostsee, so there was no danger of anyone making the same mistake as some post-war British and American historians and confusing the country between the Adriatic and the Black Sea with the Baltic. The men knew they would not be going to the Baltic and guessed they might be heading for Yugoslavia, Rumania, Albania or Greece, but no one; not even their leader had any inkling about where exactly they were heading or what they would be doing when they arrived there.

It was 27 September 1941 when this group of about thirty men set out by train, but still without the faintest clue as to where they were going. The group had been on the move for several days and was a long way past Belgrade before they were fairly certain that they could be heading towards the Mediterranean. People of that region had not been as irrational as those in Britain and had not removed signposts, so the men knew where they passed through and they could work out that they might be on a line heading

The barracks at the 3rd U-bootslehrdivision in Neustadt (Schleswig Holstein). This had very little to do with training but served as a personnel pool for people waiting for a permanent posting. This is where the initial staff for the first Mediterranean U-boat flotilla was assembled.

towards Greece. Yet, when the train came to a squeaking halt behind a hissing locomotive in the middle of nowhere, they still didn't know their destination. It was a weird place to stop; right in the middle of nowhere. The men had to walk only for a short distance along the tracks to see the reason for their premature halt. The moonlight was just about bright enough to reveal that partisans had destroyed a bridge over a deep gorge, making it necessary to climb down a path on one side and up another on the other to board another waiting train. Each man had to carry his own kitbag and also give a hand with other heavy packages, so this was not an entirely easy escapade. Kitbags may have been useful for carrying luggage onto a ship, but they were most awkward for prolonged cross-country treks. No one was quite sure whether this excursion had been timetabled for night-time to avoid the heat, local partisans or spies. Whatever the case, everybody was pleased when the train on the other side started rolling. The men were even more pleased when they arrived in Athens. There they discovered that their destination was to be Salamis, and another journey by lorry and ferry was necessary to get there.

Kptlt. Fritz Frauenheim and Oblt.z.S.(Ing.) Erich Zürn, both wearing flashy Knight's Crosses around their necks, received them there and told them they had been selected to establish the first German U-boat base in the Mediterranean. This was going to be the newly formed 23rd U-boat Flotilla. Work had to start straight away because the first U-boats were already on their way; there was no time to get acclimatised to the new surroundings. The mechanical side was well taken care of by a group of specialist workers from the large shipyard Blohm und Voss in Hamburg and from Germania Werft in Kiel. So, for the time being Kurt Sommer's group acted as gofers, working at the double to get the non-technical side going and, most important of all, to feed these essential and irreplaceable workers. The water supply, oiling installations and many of the workshops had been damaged, so there was no shortage of things requiring urgent attention.

There wasn't enough accommodation near the new base, but there had not been much action either, so the flotilla's medical centre could double up as sleeping quarters for the time being until something better could be made ready. On top of this, there were no administration offices either, so these had to be sorted as well. Food was pretty awful. It consisted mainly of rice and what the men called donkey meat because they couldn't establish what is had once been and donkeys were the main form of transport in the area. The Luftwaffe had also moved in on Salamis and it didn't take long to establish cordial relations, which involved acquiring potatoes and eggs. Since these couldn't feature on the official menu they were prepared and enjoyed during the men's free time. The big problem as far as supplies were concerned was that the Germany could not sail supply ships into the Mediterranean. Everything had to come by train from Germany and railways were not their best in wartime. Not only were there long delays but also there were no guarantees that goods would arrive.

Most of the transport between Germany and these somewhat far-off and isolated bases was by special military train. Sometimes there was enough traffic for each branch to run its own service, but they also shared trains. These were generally well organised, even during the incredible chaos at the end of the War. Each train had a special commander and enough facilities to be completely self-contained, often with its own catering staff.

Pola on the Adriatic. Looking out from naval accommodation to an airship hangar with a huge dirty cloud of some partisan activity in the far distance. This area had seen political turmoil since long before the First World War. In fact the trigger for the First World War was not far away and there were enough fighters there to have a go at anyone and everyone who interfered with their ideals in life. As a rough guide one can calculate that every fifth soldier heading east was required to protect four men in front of him from partisan attack. Sadly, the contribution made by the partisans has hardly been recognised, although some groups inflicted losses far beyond their small size and limited weapons.

A group of six U-boats had set out from France between 24 September and 5 October 1941 with specific orders to break through the Strait of Gibraltar. The famous 'Mousetrap of Gibraltar', where water currents allowed submarines to sail into the Mediterranean but made it difficult to go in the opposite direction, did not snap shut until some time later, when the Royal Navy made a determined effort to guard the passage into the Mediterranean. At this early period, there was not much need for U-boats to sail in the more difficult opposite direction. All boats of this specially prepared first wave managed to get through and their first aggressive action started on 5 October. So the men in Salamis knew that at least some of the boats had got into the Mediterranean and that the services of the new Salamis base were definitely going to be required. No one in Salamis knew which boats were likely to turn up or when they might arrive; such operational details remained secret, even to the majority of the flotilla staff.

The first boat to join the new base was U371 under Kptlt. Heinrich Driver, a standard sea-going Type VIIC, which had left Brest on the French Atlantic coast on 16 September, ten days before this group of helpers left Neustadt near Kiel. The other boats of this group, named Goeben, were: U75, U79, U97, U331 and U559.

The extra work required to deal with arriving U-boats was not the only problem in Salamis. A more human element was added by the men's search for supplements to their somewhat monotonous diet. The food did improve with time, but as a stopgap measure the men took to eating local fruit and drinking a locally made date wine. Whether this had strong laxative effects or whether the fruit was contaminated with beasties too strong for northern stomachs is difficult to establish, but the results – a massive diarrhoea outbreak – were most dramatic and incredibly incapacitating. No one could go far from a lavatory. Since the majority of the workers were still being accommodated in the small medical centre, they found themselves in the right place for such strenuous activity. Later the men were faced with other personal problems as well. The main one was created by the combination of friendly bars in cool cellars and drinking a little too much of the local brew. It tasted good, but it was like old scrumpy, without any indications that it also contained a fierce punch. Men felt perfectly all right in the coolness of the bar until they ventured out into the unforgiving sunshine. There the high temperatures had a dramatic punishing effect. It took a while before northerners got used to this combination and a number succumbed, having to be carried back to bed.

Some had it even worse and the first serious loss came on 14 March 1942. A huge crowd had assembled on the quayside to send off U133 under Kptlt. Eberhard Mohr. A tug came out to open the massive anti-submarine and anti-torpedo net. U133 nosed out to sea and shortly afterwards, while the crowd was still watching, ran into what was probably the remains of an old Greek minefield. The detonation was so strong that the boat vanished within a few seconds and afterwards the sea was as calm as it had been before the huge blast. There were no survivors. Kurt Sommer wrote that men quay stood there as if paralysed, with tears in their eyes.

The Mediterranean theatre grew in importance and in such voracity that more bases had to be established. The limited facilities in Salamis just couldn't cope with the demand, so in June 1942 a number of the old hands from Salamis were moved to establish additional facilities in La Spezia. Although this was an important undertaking, the transport provided was not what the men had expected. Finding the necessary railway carriages was not easy, so the move was made with everything and everybody travelling in cattle trucks. The journey via Salonika, Belgrade, Zagreb, Klagenfurt and Verona to La Spezia took about two weeks.

Otto Wagner was a Verwaltungsmaat (Petty Administration Officer), whose main job was the procurement of food for the Salamis U-boat base. He was working there during the middle of September 1944 and had just left it with a lorry when more than a hundred American bombers attacked. Getting back into the base after the raid with a lorry full of food turned out to be a problem. A huge crater, all the way across the main approach, prevented further progress and the smouldering ruins beyond it suggested that the catering branch definitely needed to find new kitchen. The chaos left behind in the mess (dining room) was also going to take a while to sort out. This was well in hand when the second large raid came a day or so later. This time the opposition was more obliging by dropping most of the bombs into the water and leaving the catering facilities untouched. However, the harbour and the dockyard were no longer in the best of condition. The power of exploding bombs looked nowhere near as dramatic as is shown in modern films, but their effects were often considerably more astonishing. In St Nazaire, for example, a car was blown off the street to rest in the attic on top of four floors of office space. This time, in Salamis, one patrol boat disappeared completely, another one was left lying in a road and two U-boats were buckled on the side of the blast, rendering them more or less useless. It looked as if the wrecked remains of the shipyard were not going to cope with the repairs for the time being. So the U-boats were scuttled a short time later. In any case, the total number of U-boats in the Mediterranean was being drastically reduced due to intensive enemy action; by this time, that is the middle of September 1944, there was only one left. The rapidly deteriorating situation in the hinterland made it clear that the U-boat bases would need to be evacuated.

Civilian employees came under the same military jurisdiction as soldiers and therefore were not free to leave when they wanted to. Instead everybody had to wait for evacuation orders. Anyone found travelling without the necessary papers would be looked upon as a deserter, a crime punishable by instant execution. Remaining in Greece was becoming noticeably more difficult by the day, with partisan operations striking in new weak spots without the army of occupation being able to stop them. Everything of use to the Germans was systematically destroyed, to encourage the remaining garrisons to leave. Yet, withdrawing was not terribly easy. Naval uniforms were burned while almost everything else surplus to requirements was traded for food or left for the locals. Despite the problems on the mainland and in Athens, there was relatively little trouble in the U-boat base, perhaps a reflection of the reasonable cooperation, which had existed between the German Navy and local businesses.

The U-boat base was eventually evacuated during the afternoon of 2 October 1944. A lighter took the men to the mainland and from there they went by lorry to the railway station, which was already bursting with soldiers, all anxious to get back to Germany. In and around the station there were also several hundred civilians, many of them Greeks and foreigners from surrounding countries, trying to get tickets for a journey to Germany. Both the Red Army and the local partisans had acquired a reputation of metering out the most horrendous torture to people they captured. Many were eager to avoid such severe retribution. The German occupation of Greece was particularly bloody, there can be no denying that; but today the media keeps telling us about the marvellous liberation without mentioning the masses of people who had to suffer dreadful punishment before being murdered.

Despite the crowded and somewhat chaotic situation, the planning seems to have been pretty good and the train did eventually get underway. However, no one could have anticipated the hardship of that journey, or that it would take three whole months to reach it destination. Partisan activity was so great that at one stage progress was made only by a German soldier holding a pistol to the chest of a driver to force him into coupling up his engine to make the train roll on. Wherever the train came to, the men found new problems preventing them from making further progress. There were well over 600 people aboard and just keeping them fed and watered was an incredibly difficult juggling act. Progress was slow, but the train did eventually get within 70 miles or so of Belgrade, the capital of the former Yugoslavia. There, while waiting at a station, the men were horrified to see that a train coming the other way riddled with holes made by machine gun bullets. The commander of the special train, with the men from the U-boat base at Salamis on board, a Luftwaffe Colonel, refused to continue, saying he would have to face a court martial if there was a noteworthy loss of life.

As it happened, the German administration appeared to have been efficient enough to send an armoured train with considerable hitting power to go ahead and, if necessary, blast a way through any ambushes. All this didn't get the men much further; a few miles on they discovered that Russian forces had already crossed the line ahead of them. Therefore they had to stop and await new orders. In the end there was no choice other than to go back, to find another way around the Russian spearhead. Both the Russians and the partisans were making excellent progress, creating considerable difficulties when it came to working out which routes might still be available for a train containing six hundred people. Communications had all but broken down and passengers got used to waiting. Otto Wagner was doing his best to help out as cook for what remained of the Salamis U-boat base and felt most despondent because a large number of officers left the train to make their own way back to Germany. It certainly looked as if this was going to be the easy option for dealing with the advancing Russians and partisans. However, while officers might manage to explain their reasons for leaving the train, men from the U-boat base could be looked upon as deserters and might end up being executed by the first German troops they meet.

Luckily the train did make slow progress through what was such highly impoverished country that the men found they could easily trade their unwanted items for food. The tropical gear many had with them was no longer required and was easily exchanged for locally grown produce. The nights were already getting noticeably colder and it wasn't long before snow hampered further progress. Eventually it did come to walking, something the men of the navy weren't prepared for at all. They didn't have the necessary footwear for long treks over torturous terrain and, secondly, walking long distances was something they had not done for several years. Blisters and a variety of other minor, but painful injuries, slowed progress to a crawl. Despite these severe difficulties, military discipline was still ruling the roost and even this troubled evacuation was reasonably well organised. The men walked because there was no transport, but luggage was placed aboard lorries, horses, mules and donkeys so that, at least, they didn't have to carry too much. The medical service was still active as well and selected the men with the worst injuries were carried aboard the trucks.

Although food was not plentiful, there was enough, and at night accommodation was found in either houses or in tents. Acquiring the food was not easy and the group, still under its military leadership, came to a halt at frequent intervals so that one lorry could go off to collect provisions. The further the men travelled, the more chaotic the general situation became. They ran into horrendous scenes of poverty and dereliction with the roads and settlements looking dirty and primitive as if from a bygone age. Yet progress continued throughout the winter. Finally, in mid January, these men from the Salamis U-boat base arrived at a naval base in Plön (Schleswig Holstein). In Britain people tend to look back and refer to this action as having been a glorious liberation and many have forgotten the horrors of the time. These were so awful that if these stories were written in a novel, then readers would classify them as too far-fetched.

Towards the end of the War, partisans in the east and groups from the French Resistance in the west presented a considerable problem for unarmed Germans attempting a cross-country run back to Germany. The five serviceable U-boats in the Black Sea were not allowed to attempt an underwater escape through the Bosporus because of an assurance given by the German government to respect Turkey's neutrality and a considerable number of well-armed partisan groups made it impractical for their crews to retreat westwards overland. As a result the men unable to walk were set ashore with provisions in isolated locations so that they could lie low for a few days. The boats were then scuttled and the remaining members of the crew attempted to make their way through Turkey to hopefully reach the Mediterranean. The initial plan was to steal boats there for sailing to a German port along the Adriatic coast. Of course, none of them men got terribly far and most ended up as prisoners to be interned, but with the happy thought that they had survived both the War and the onslaught of vicious partisan attacks.

CHAPTER 9
Far-Away Bases

WILHELMSHAVEN SÜD (SOUTH) IN THE SOUTH ATLANTIC

Although used in communications as codename, Wilhelmshaven-South was an unofficial nickname for the British freighter *Duquesa*, belonging to Furness and Holder of Liverpool. The heavy cruiser *Admiral Scheer* captured her in December 1940, a few miles north of the Equator, while she was on her way back to Britain with a full load of provisions, including thousands of eggs. A few weeks earlier *Duquesa* survived a massive air raid on London docks. Another ship in the same basin was not so lucky and went down after it had been blown away from its berth. The gap remaining between this sunken vessel and the lock gates was just wide enough for the *Duquesa* to squeeze through to start a voyage to South America, where her refrigerated holds were filled with valuable supplies.

Admiral Scheer was not alone in the South Atlantic when she captured *Duquesa* and several auxiliary cruisers, as well as submarines, were supplied for several weeks from this most welcome source. The bonanza continued until the coal-burning freighter ran out of fuel; then it was kept going a little longer by burning furniture and fittings to maintain the power for the refrigeration plant. Eventually, when the tropical heat ensured that the food started going bad, the ship was scuttled. During its time in German hands *Duquesa* supplied enough food and eggs for the majority of recipients to be thoroughly fed up with having to eat them in every possible combination the cooks could dream up. All these supply operations took place on the high seas, so there was never a land-based Wilhelmshaven-South.

THE FAR EAST

The main German centres in the Far East were:

Japan:
Tokyo	Naval Attaché at the German Embassy
Kobe	Used Japanese naval base
Yokohama	Used Japanese naval base

Malaya:

Penang	Planned as and used as main German U-boat base
Singapore	A Japanese base with German naval staff. (Shonan in wartime German and Shonanto in Japanese)

Java:

Surabaya	Japanese base with German naval staff
Djakarta	Japanese base with German naval staff (officially known as Batavia until 1942)

Shonan Island – Singapore

The following extracts come from a small booklet given to German soldiers when they arrived in Singapore. This information has been supplemented with details from Otto Giese and with information from the book he has written with Captain James Wise, details of which are in the Bibliography. The wording of the original booklet has been kept to maintain the flavour of the times.

The German official offices in Penang with high power radio transmitter in the raised central section of the house.

The Elysee Hotel and cinema in Penang used to accommodate German U-boat crews. The Germans were particularly keen on finding buildings with efficient air conditioning.

Kriegsmarine Base Singapore
The German headquarters are in the Union Building on the 4th and 5th Floors. The building is situated on the seafront near Quay 12.
Other German naval accommodation is at:
House No. 1   Gilstead Road 25
House No. 2   Gilstead Road 31
House No. 3   Gilstead Road 39
House No. 4   Newton Road 23

House No. 4 is occupied by the Officer Commanding German Naval Offices in Malaya and by the Officer in Command of the German Naval Base – Singapore.

In addition to the above, there are the following facilities at the Pasir Panjang Camp by the seafront on the Pasir Panjang Road.

Warehouse 1
Warehouse 2
Dockyard Command Store
House for Officer in Charge of the Stores

The Tiger Club for officers in Singapore. (*Photo: Otto Giese*)

Officer accommodation
Soldiers' hostel
Tiger House – Officers' club [Owned by the Chinese manufacturer of Tiger Balm, an ointment for curing almost anything and most popular at the time.]

The Imperial Japanese Navy provides all the buildings and it is the duty of every man to maintain both the houses and the items inside them. Anyone who breaks anything or damages property will be harming his fellow colleagues who come to occupy these properties after him. Consideration for others is essential.

Behaviour
There are very close ties of friendship between Japanese and German soldiers and it is essential that everybody maintains this healthy state of affairs. The German soldier is expected to remain restrained, to adapt and to fit in. It is important to bear in mind that Japan is our only strong and true partner and Germany is Japan's only strong and true ally.

Conduct outside the military camps must set an example to others and be exemplary all the time. The behaviour of one person will reflect on the whole German nation. It is essential that everybody is especially careful and reserved when dealing with natives or when forming relationships with them. Forming close friendships with natives or taking them into your confidence is disgraceful. Full secrecy must be maintained all the time.

It is essential to wear a badge so that the local police can instantly identify you as German. The Naval Office will issue these identification tags. It goes without mentioning that every soldier, whether in uniform or in civilian clothing, must always look clean and tidy.

Time off within the Naval Base
Anyone going on leave in Singapore will be expected to comply with local base regulations. Anyone breaking these rules will have his free time severely curtailed and offenders must also expect serious punishment.

Food
The Naval Office tries hard to provide a varied diet, but it is essential to realise that the food available is not the same as in Germany. There are considerable transport problems and some items are frequently in short supply.

Thieving
There have been cases where things have gone missing from the accommodation areas and it is important to emphasise that every person is responsible for his own property. Money and any valuable items should be handed in to the Division's Officer who will make sure they are kept safely under lock and key.

Emergency Medical Help
A German doctor will deal with all medical problems, if one happens to be available. If not, it will be necessary to make use of the facilities in the local Naval Hospital. Whatever happens, all illnesses and injuries must be reported immediately to the German Command Office.

Health
The tropical climate harbours a number of dangers as far as health is concerned and everybody is expected to take extra care. It is essential to be careful when eating and drinking, and to take precautions not to catch unnecessary colds. The slightest carelessness can produce serious results, the grimmest of which are sexually transmitted diseases and a number of intestinal complaints such as dysentery, typhoid and cholera. Drinking un-boiled water or eating ice is strictly prohibited. Consuming food from roadside stalls or unknown restaurants is not allowed. Fresh fruit must be washed with safe water before it is eaten. Washing hands before every meal is essential to prevent any transmission of diseases. Local alcoholic drinks contain a high proportion of methyl alcohol, which is most damaging to health. It affects the brain and the eyes and can result in permanent blindness.

Prostitution is widespread and there are no controls over girls when they go home. A shortage of medicines has resulted in a variety of sexually transmitted diseases being rampant. This means that every girl has got to be considered to be a health risk. Infection is certain for anyone indulging in sexual activities without condoms and without taking the necessary preventative medicines. So far about 10% of soldiers have caught sexually transmitted diseases.

Shopping

Singapore's main shopping area can be reached easily on foot from the navy's accommodation, making shopping easy, but the prices have rocketed in recent months. Soap, other toilet articles and leather, especially shoes, have gone up considerably. In view of this it is important to compare prices from a variety of shops before buying anything. Men from the German Command Centre stationed here are always willing to help and to give advice about making purchases. Some items are controlled and rationed, which means acquiring them is not too easy and one must avoid contact with black marketers, who sell at incredibly inflated prices. When buying shoes it is important to select a pair with rubber soles. Soles from locally produced leather are often not able to withstand the heavy rain.

Transport

A shortage of spare parts and hardly any repair facilities means that getting about is not easy and can be rather frustrating at times. There are no alternatives to using the few vehicles supplied by the Japanese Navy and it is expected that these will treated with the utmost respect. All vehicles come with local drivers, who know the routes and are able to cope with the traffic in town.

Any questions should be directed to the Transport Officer in the base. The best way of getting about is by local bus and in town one can use rickshaws. [Rickshaws became a bone of contention between the Japanese and the Germans. Rich owners hired these out to poor operators who often had no real home and slept in their rickshaw. Feeling sorry for them and wanting to alleviate the poverty, the Germans started paying considerably more than the prices asked. The Japanese objected most fervently because this helped to drive up the price of travel in town.] Taxis are limited and fares often terribly expensive. To prevent any misunderstandings, one should establish the price with the driver before starting any journey.

Stopping cars to ask for a lift or thumbing lifts is strictly prohibited and anyone who goes against this rule will be severely dealt with. It is far too easy to create misunderstanding with members of the Japanese Navy or Army and any such incident must be avoided at all cost.

Saluting

When wearing uniform it is necessary to salute according to one's rank:
1. All Japanese officers and warrant officers from all military services.
2. All vehicles with yellow, red or blue flags. (Yellow indicates an admiral or general, red a staff officer and blue a lieutenant or lieutenant commander.)

Bars and Restaurants
You are allowed to visit any bar or restaurant but if possible the following should be used because the Japanese authorities have approved these. [Note that this contradicts an earlier comment. There followed a long list of clubs, bars and dance halls for officers only, warrant officers and others for all ranks.] All Japanese bars are labelled with a prominent 'M'.

In addition to Japanese films, cinemas show predominantly Malaysian and Chinese films. Other places of special interest are: The Shonan Museum known as the Raffles Museum in earlier days, the botanic gardens and the Shinto Temple. Journeys to Johore are possible and take about an hour. Such long trips are best planned as group activities by each individual command.

Sport
Details will be provided upon arrival. Generally it is possible to swim, play handball or football, table tennis and tennis and one can indulge in gymnastics on the lawns of individual houses.

[End of the German Booklet.]

Additional Allied Information
It would seem that the Allied intelligence departments were keen to discover details of the German bases in foreign countries and even produced booklets with information gleaned from prisoners of war. Obviously this was also laced with as much sensitive propaganda as could be squeezed in and therefore it is now difficult to work out how much of this was based on facts rather than stories from propaganda departments. The following comes one such Allied account about Batavia or Djakarta.

Air Raids
None of the German crews experienced air raids, but they did find themselves caught up in air raid practises and were forced to spend considerable time, often several hours on end, in one of the many ditches and shelters built for this purpose. The local police was polite but most firm that everybody, including visiting German crews, obeyed the rules and regulations.

Curfew
Japanese troops had to be in their bases by 20.00 hours, but bars and restaurants remained open until 23.00 hours when the local population and officers also had to be indoors.

Prostitution
Djakarta had similar rules to Singapore but German officers were not allowed to visit brothels set aside for Japanese officers. Apparently some European women were forced to work in brothels for some time until protests from the United States

put an end to such practices. [Looking at these words in retrospect, it is strange that the Japanese authorities should bow to American demands at this time and one wonders whether the sentence was added merely to make Allied soldiers think they were indeed serving an influential power.]

There was no shortage of prostitutes in official bars and in the streets, although the health warnings given to soldiers in Singapore applied in Djakarta as well. Some Germans reported that there were a great many half-cast girls living in the most pitiful conditions under the Japanese administration. Wartime shortages, together with a general breakdown of the economic situation meant that many of them had to sell personal belongings in order to buy basic necessities such as food.

It would appear that counter-espionage was almost non-existent in the Far Eastern bases and it seemed likely that many of these girls supplied information to Allied intelligence systems. Otto Giese remarked that this seemed to have been highly likely. Sensitive information, such as the times when U-boats departed didn't appear to have been highly secret. Many were attacked shortly after leaving port or while on their way into a Japanese base. Many Germans were astonished by the wide military knowledge of many girls and of some locals with whom they came into daily contact.

The Far Eastern Naval Supply System

The German Kaiser established a Naval Attaché at the Embassy in Tokyo and this office was set up again a few years after the First World War. The position was occupied by Kpt.z.S. Paul Wenneker from December 1933 until the end of 1937 when he became commanding officer of the pocket battleship *Deutschland*. *Deutschland* was sent to sea before the beginning of the Second World War and remained in the North Atlantic until December 1939. On returning from his first war voyage, Wenneker was sent back to Tokyo to continue with the work he had started some years earlier. The journey was comparatively easy during that early war period because a friendship pact between Germany and Russia made it possible to obtain transit visas for the Siberian Railway, which took passengers as far as the Pacific coast.

One of Wenneker's first aims was to help blockade breakers (ordinary cargo ships running through the British blockade) attempt voyages back to Europe. Later he was also called upon to assist with ghost cruiser operations. Preparing both supply ships and blockade breakers for voyages to Europe was made easier by Germany having a most efficient radio network. The first long-distance telephone lines were established under the British Empire and, not wanting to be dependent on these, Imperial Germany developed radio systems for keeping in touch with its colonies. This made it possible to arrange for coal to be supplied to the light cruiser *Emden* during the First World War and enabled the ship to carry on with its highly successful raiding programme. Radio communications had improved to such an extent that during the Second World War the German Naval Staff in Berlin was able to keep in touch with ships on far-distant seas. In some cases it was even possible for ships in neutral ports to use their radios for making arrangements to return home with valuable war goods.

Martin Brice's book *Axis Blockade Runners of World War II* (Blockadebrecher – see Bibliography) states that a total of over 112,000 tons of raw materials were imported from the Far East and that almost half of this was made up of rubber. In return Germany exported almost 57,000 tons of machinery, chemicals and technical samples to Japan, involving well over one hundred ships. So the traffic between either Germany or the German occupied ports of the French Biscay coast and foreign, mainly Far Eastern, ports was quite considerable.

THE SPECIAL NAVAL SERVICE (MARINESONDERDIENST)

At the beginning of the Second World War, there were a vast number of German or German-friendly shipping offices around the globe. These supplied ships with cargoes and with any other items asked for. Shopping lists for consumables aboard ships were usually sent by radio long before the ship arrived in a port so that the necessary materials could be purchased at a reasonable price and at a suitable quality. These were then stored at a portside warehouse until the recipient was ready to take them on board. This acquisition process was quite involved and as made worse by the comparatively large quantities required by ships.

Long before the War, the German Naval High Command put resources aside to establish a military branch for such a specialised supply network and this eventually became known as the Special Naval Service (Marinesonderdienst). Since the beginning of the Second World War it came under the leadership of Kpt.z.S. Werner Vermehren, who was based in Japan, although the actual headquarters were later in Bordeaux (France). This most remarkable character was born in El Paso (Texas) and joined the Imperial Navy in 1909 as an officer candidate and later made a considerable contribution to keeping German shipping running under incredibly difficult circumstances. Naval attachés, who had a number of specialised officers to help them for this specific task, controlled the organisation. Once the War started, it became quickly apparent that the main supply source was going to be in Japan or territories nearby and many of the other offices slowly disappeared from the scene. The British and American influence in many neutral countries was too great for German activities to continue with any significant crescendo. Yet, some merchant ships, especially *Rio Grande* made several voyages from France to South America. Sadly the contribution made by the Marinesonderdienst is now largely forgotten and hardly mentioned by the majority of historians.

GERMAN COLONIES

The First World War had hardly started when both the Allied powers and many neutral countries made a concerted effort to curtail German interests in foreign territories. As a result many trading links established before the War were quickly cut. After the War, Germany was in such a pitiful state that it was not difficult for foreign powers, once friendly with Germany, to be persuaded to switch their allegiance. In any case Germany did not have deep-rooted interests in foreign countries. The German acquisition of foreign colonies started relatively late with the African colonies not being acquired until the 1880s, and they were all given up again by the time the First World War ended. Although there were German territories in West Africa, in South-West Africa and East Africa, none of the coastal towns had natural harbours. A few warships were stationed in foreign waters as far away as Chile, but Germany had only one significant naval base in foreign lands. This was at Tsingtau in China, which it lost shortly after the beginning of the First War.

This modest colonial expansion did result in centres of German interest being dotted around the globe; some of this was rekindled once the National Socialists restored pride in the country. In addition to these small colonial communities, additional new cores of German interest started growing as a result of Germans being marooned in foreign countries as a result of the Second World War. Freighters, some of them with a good number of passengers on board, had no alternative other than to seek shelter in far-off neutral countries. A few days before the beginning of the Second World War German merchant ships were advised to run into a German port within four days and if this was not possible to seek shelter in the nearest neutral country. Some of these were more neutral than others and ships were warned to avoid possible hostile places, especially the United States. Eager to enter the War as well, the United States commenced with aggressive action against Germany as soon as Europe started shooting and it was not long before United States forces made concerted efforts to trail German ships and pass details of their positions on to British warships. As a result a number of merchant ships, including the passenger liner *Columbus*, had to be scuttled to prevent them from falling into British hands.

TSINGTAU – KIAUTSCHOU

Tsingtau was the port at Kiatschou in China where the German Far Eastern Naval Squadron was stationed until the beginning of the First World War and it is included here because the Kiautschou Barracks are still standing in Cuxhaven near the U-boat Museum as legacy of the period. This complex was opened in April 1909 to train all types of personnel for service in China. An entire coastal artillery unit, in those days still called Matrosenartillerie (Sailors' Artillery) was moved from Wilhelmshaven with the specific aim of training the men to cope with life in foreign countries. The 552 square kilometres of land at Kiautschou were leased for ninety-nine years from China in 1898 and occupied by Japan and other powers shortly after the start of the First World War. Japanese forces interned the remaining Germans and the Allies saw to it that German interests in the territory were denounced. In 1922 the area was handed back to China.

Originally the area consisted of nothing more than a chain of fishing villages around what was a grand natural harbour. Germany developed this sheltered area to become a vast port with all facilities ships might require, including a dry dock. The governor of the colony was a serving naval officer whose immediate superior was always the Kaiser himself, without interference from the Naval High Command or from Fleet interests. It did not take long before the smattering of natives increased to some 200,000 plus 5,000 Europeans in the new town of Tsingtau. The governor was supported by the Third Sea Battalion from the German Navy. This had a strength of about 1,200 men. In addition, there were also some 200 specialists from the naval artillery (still matrosenartillerie in those days) to operate a number of large-calibre guns in fixed defensive positions along the harbour approaches. Later, when the outbreak of the War led to the withdrawal of ships from China, these forces were considerably strengthened, mainly with men evacuated from other parts of China.

Tsingtau was the main base for the German Far East Cruiser Squadron, under command of Reichsgraf Maximilian von Spee at the outbreak of the First World War. This consisted of the two heavy cruisers *Scharnhorst* (flagship) and *Gneisenau* plus the three small cruisers, *Emden*, *Leipzig* and *Nürnberg*, and the supply ship *Titania*. In addition to these, there were also a number of small gunboats for coastal or river employment, but none of them big enough to attempt a run back to Europe. The light cruiser *Dresden*, based at the German South American Naval Station in Chile, joined this group in an attempt to get back to Germany at the outbreak of the War. The German cruiser squadron won a major battle at Coronel off the western coast of South America when it engaged a British squadron on 1 November 1914, but the Germans were later annihilated at the Battle of the Falklands. Only the *Dresden* managed to escape, to hide for some time in the myriad of deep-water inlets of the Fireland or Tierra del Fuego. The light cruiser *Emden* was the last ship to leave Tsingtau on 5 August 1914 with permission to conduct its own cruiser war against merchant shipping in the Pacific and Indian Oceans. This was made possible because German ships were equipped with the most advanced radio sets and therefore were able to coordinate supplies and coaling ships to keep the cruiser active. *Emden*'s endeavours were most remarkable and after the sinking of the ship, the landing detachment even managed to make its own way home against the highest odds. These achievements were so remarkable that the Kaiser decreed that all of *Emden*'s men were to add the name of their ship to their own surname and even today one still finds remnants of these families. The Second World War U-boat Commander Hans-Jürgen Lauterbach-Emden is just one example.

Another, hardly known yet most remarkable character in Tsingtau at the beginning of the War was a pilot, Oblt.z.S. Gunther Plüschow, who managed to escape together with his aircraft and later helped to reconnoitre the still mysterious water channels of the South American continent.

Tsingtau developed into a thriving seaport in just sixteen years, not only with the usual maritime facilities but also with a university and other trading provisions. There was a railway and the place became recognized as the healthiest part of China with a contrasting climate, but still nowhere near as extreme as in the hotter southern regions.

U-boats Refuelling in Spain

It is no longer a secret that German U-boats were re-fuelled in neutral Spain and that some ships stopped off there during the War to seek shelter in its neutral harbours. Such emergency stop-offs were technically legal according to international agreements as long as the ship called for the purpose of seeking medical aid for its men and did not take any provisions on board which could help it in future combat. Both sides of any conflict had their own representatives in most likely ports to ensure that their own nation's interests were looked after and to make sure that the opposition didn't gain any advantages from their stay in foreign neutral ports. Yet, despite both sides watching each other, it was often possible to smuggle small quantities of essential war materials. At one time, for example, the German Naval Attaché visited a stranded U-boat with piston rings for the engine hidden inside his trouser legs.

Some of the re-fuelling places were identified by codenames, known only to very few people; working out their exact locations appears to be almost impossible these days, unless one happens to stumble accidentally upon a correct key to the problem. The search for such refuelling bases is made worse by a vast multitude of strange stories about U-boats landing in foreign ports, but with hardly any of them based on fact.

German Naval Bases in North Russia

If the concept of German bases in northern Russia comes over as an absurd joke then it is necessary to remember that the two countries had a common border until the end of the First World War. The land on both sides of this line was sparsely inhabited and the ordinary people living along it got on very well, despite the Czars having introduced a cumbersome bureaucratic system long before other European nations made it necessary to have passports for moving from one country to another. The reasonably close relationships with Russia were rekindled during the early 1930s, when negotiations started with the planning of the German Basis Nord in the Fjord of Litza some 25 kilometres west of Murmansk, and at Teriberka, some 50 kilometres to the east.

Finding information about these developments with the name Basis Nord (Northern Base) is not easy, despite the project having been mentioned by a number of reliable authors. It would appear that not many facts have come to light and those in this book are based on details from Lars Westerlund at the National Archives in Finland. The German U-boat Archive in Cuxhaven-Altenbruch would be delighted if anyone could contribute more information, especially details from the British side.

The major problem with this Arctic activity was that it started growing early, when exploration of the Polar ice was still very much in its infancy and the necessity to have a base in those barren waters dwindled dramatically during the spring of 1940, when Germany gained access to the deeply incised Norwegian coast. It would seem that the development of dockyards in Russia continued almost until the end of that year because the officer responsible for the construction was not moved to pastures new until October

1940. This was the forty-year old Fregattenkapitän (Ing.) Karl Nieschlag from Lehrte near Hannover, who then became leader of the Kriegsmarine Werft in Bordeaux. Records of what he established during his 10-month-spell in northern Russia are more than sparse and trying to find the exact location of his activities is also difficult because both areas have a number of small centres with rudimentary ship repairing facilities. That northern coast was so isolated that it needn't have existed as far as naval record keepers were concerned, but despite this, there is evidence that a number of ships called in northern Russia towards the beginning of the War. The problem is that these could have sought refuge in one of the thousands of safe fiords or bays, and trying to unravel exactly which ships did go up there is just as difficult as tracing the exact location of their destination. Unfortunately this activity took place before the British deciphering centre could read much of the German secret radio code and Bletchley Park decryptions are unlikely to provide the same rich information as they can with boats going to the Far East.

Naval Records also mention a Sonderkommando Nord, but this almost certainly had no connection with the activities in northern Russia. It would seem that this name appeared for the first time towards the end of the War to cover U-boat activities in the northern Baltic, especially in Finnish waters.

THE GERMAN U-BOAT BUNKER IN ENGLAND

It is hardly known that a huge, four-bay U-boat bunker was built in a top-secret location right in the heart of England. The nearest bit of water was a 6-inch deep stream, so it was unlikely that any unit of the German Navy would ever reach it, but the bombs used to tackle the huge U-boat shelters towards the end of the War did get close. This incredible structure was part of the Ashley Walk Bombing Range in the New Forest, a few miles south of the Fordingbridge – Brook road and only a few yards south of Pitts Wood. Details of the exact location can be found on the Internet, if one searches under Ashley Walk Bombing Range.

The story of this almost unknown but most remarkable bunker started around the beginning of the War, when several thousand acres of sparsely inhabited, open moorland was fenced in to become a testing station for all manner of explosives delivered by aircraft. Being a testing station rather than a mere weapons-range meant that the targets constructed there had to resemble the real things and many valuable items, such as the armour decking of battleships, were salvaged again after the War for recycling. The high secrecy surrounding the tests on this range has resulted in only a few of the details being preserved and there were a number of structures on the site that are difficult to identify. In addition to this, it is rather sad that there appear to be only a small number of surviving photographs. However, we do know that the replica of a German U-boat bunker and the steel battleship were used as targets for Barnes Wallis's deep penetration bombs.

Barnes Wallis is probably most famous for having designed the Wellington bomber and then the bouncing 'Dam Busters' bomb, but after that he also invented and built a number of deep-penetration bombs. There were three of these, the 22,000-lb Grand Slam,

The only known German wartime submarine bunker in the United Kingdom was located in the New Forest where it was used to test Barnes Wallis's revolutionary bunker-breaking bombs. After the War, the eyesore was covered with soil, and trees were allowed to grow over it. Details of this location can be found on the Internet under Ashley Bombing Range.

a 12,000-lb Tallboy and a smaller, experimental model of about 4,000 lbs. The original idea was to drop the two big ones from a height of about 35,000 feet, but the largest bomber of the time, the Lancaster, could carry only one bomb at a time to a maximum of 18,000 feet. The idea was to drop them by the side of concrete fortifications so that the bomb would bury itself deep in the ground before exploding and then create an earthquake-like shuddering to break the structure above it. The bombs themselves were made from thick high-quality steel and manufactured to exceedingly accurate technical specifications. This was mainly to ensure that they were perfectly streamlined to rotate while falling without wobbling off course. This worked well and at least six live Tallboys plus several bombs without explosives inside them were dropped on the Ashley Range to see how well they could deal with reinforced concrete.

In addition to being highly secret, the bunker became an obvious rectangular eyesore on the top of the hill and after the War it was covered with soil to make it blend in with its surroundings. This mound is now overgrown with lush vegetation, but bits of concrete can still be seen in a few places. Even more interesting, there is what could well be the only remaining perfectly round Tallboy crater nearby. This is now full of water and looks so much like a Victorian farm pond that the majority of people passing it would probably not recognise it for what it is.

Towards the end of the War, bombers carrying special earthquake bombs attacked the concrete installations of the main German naval bases. It would appear that the only surviving crater made by such a heavy and precision-engineered weapon is this one on the testing range in the New Forest. It now looks very much like a natural Dewpond.

Not much remains of Barnes Wallis's bombs. The Brooklands Museum in Surrey (England), on the site of the old racetrack where Wallis used to work, has a set of these bombs on display. Even more impressive are the remains of an exploded example kept in the U-boat bunker Valentin at Farge near Bremen. This shows the incredible thickness of the steel and one can also inspect holes in the roof made by the bombs, albeit most of them in tests after the War. Both Tallboys and Grand Slams had unique tail fins, which looked as if the fixed blades were detached from the main shell of the bomb. After the War the Royal Air Force developed the Blue Danube atomic bomb with similar dimensions and these can be distinguished by having part of the tail fins retractable so that Vulcan bombers could throw them more easily. Such bombs are also on display in a few museums with labels saying they are either Tallboys or Grand Slams.

CHAPTER 10
Naval Artillery and Naval Infantry

Men from the naval artillery, with the initials MA (Marineartillerie) after their rank, may not have had any naval experience at all and possibly had never set foot on anything that floated. Others progressed from this land-based section to the sea-going side and after a little training were even given the command of a sea-going ship. A good example is Kptlt. Hans-Joachim Rahmlow, who joined the navy in 1928, five years before Hitler came to power. At the beginning of the War he was a company commander with the naval artillery and served as Commander of 4th and later with the 10th Ersatz Marineartillerieabteilung until March 1940, when he started his U-boat training. In November of that year he was given his first command (U58) and shortly after that, in May 1941, a brand new U-boat (U570). This he surrendered to an aircraft in mid-Atlantic just three months later, handing the Royal Navy a most valuable prize. Moving in the opposite direction, from sea-going to naval artillery, seems easier to explain when one bears in mind that injuries sometimes prevented men with good qualifications from serving aboard ships.

It should be considered that men unfit for service at sea could still be wearing naval blue uniforms while working in a wide variety of positions in the naval bases. Entry requirements for coastal artillery were more relaxed and men medically unfit for going to sea or above the maximum age for joining were still accepted for the naval artillery.

Anyone delving into the history of the land-based naval branches will soon get lost in a multitude of names because there appear to have been a number of different divisions, all with similar sounding titles. For example, there was the Marinebataillon, Seebataillon, Marinedivision, Marinekorps, Marineinfanterie and so forth. However, anyone specialising in modern history will be pleased to know that the last of these was phased out during the 1920s as a result of the Treaty of Versailles, and none of them were active by the time the Second World War started.

The biggest and probably most important group wearing field grey uniforms was the naval artillery, which had roots going back further than 1877 when a number of Sea Artillery Detachments were amalgamated to form an autonomous organisation then called Sailor Artillery (Matrosenartillerie). At that time the Sea Artillery Groups were focusing on firmer land-based activities by giving up one of their main weapons; large rowing boats, each with a cannon on board. This transformation highlights the tremendous changes taking place as a result of the mechanisation created by the industrial revolution.

Sea Artillery Branches had originally been founded some twenty years earlier by the army hiving off four officers and less than 150 men for specific coastal protection duties and attaching them to the Sea Battalion in Danzig. This Sea Battalion came into being under similar circumstances to the British Royal Marines, with the men under direct command of the ship's commander. In addition to manning guns, their duties included the guarding of ships, leading landing parties, keeping unruly sailors under control and so forth.

In 1877 the First Brigade of the Matrosenartillerie was established in Friedrichsort (Kiel) close to where the locks of the Kiel Canal are now situated, and the Second Brigade set up shop in Wilhelmshaven; both with the main aim of recruiting men with naval backgrounds for shooting heavy guns at moving targets. The name was later changed to Marineartillerie and the men had the letters MA added after their rank, so that they should not be confused with sea-going personnel. In addition to enlarging the setup, another branch was established later with the new name of Marineflakartillerie, to specialise in shooting down airships and aircraft. Much of this collapsed in 1918 due to the limitations imposed by the Treaty of Versailles, and Germany had to seriously re-think its coastal defence plans. Many military installations had to be dismantled and coastal defences with guns of more than 105-mm could not be upgraded. In addition to this, manpower had to be reduced so drastically that the navy were hardly able to man what remained of the fleet.

The post-war rethinking of the coastal defence strategy was not easy. Peace may have broken out in Europe during November 1918 but six months later the newly formed country of Poland attacked Russia in an attempt to move its frontier further east; there were also powerful Polish voices calling for further expansion in the west. The general unrest that remained, the fear of more land being seized by Poland and the reported atrocities being committed against Germans who refused to hand over their homes, possessions and businesses was most disturbing. Germany was in such a run-down state that there was little the government could do to ease the situation. The only comforting thought for the navy was that the newly created Poland had neither a naval base nor a navy with which it could threaten the west. However, these were not long in coming; a naval dockyard was being built in Gdynia (Gotenhafen) and ships were also being assembled. Yet, despite this, the threat from the air was far more of a concern than having to fend off any attack from the sea.

The arguments flying around Germany immediately after the First World War were extreme and included such suggestions as doing away with the navy altogether and making it part of the army. When this was rejected there was further fierce debate about the type of ships to build and this is where coastal artillery made an interesting contribution, being considerably cheaper than a ship carrying the equivalent firepower. Yet the Treaty of Versailles prevented Germany from building new coastal defence batteries with large guns, so this part of the programme remained in a state of flux. Since Germany was so severely restricted by the limitations of the Versailles Treaty, it was felt important to concentrate on this multi-purpose aspect and also to make every effort to improve automation, gun-aiming and fire-control systems.

In the end the navy settled for keeping the two distinct divisions within the naval artillery. By 1926 there existed seven major naval artillery detachments as follows: I Kiel,

There were a number of standard bunker designs, manned by the army, air force or navy, but the daily duties ran along similar lines no matter who was manning them. The majority of the men were allowed to stand down once routine duties had been completed, to take it easy. Then only a few were required to be armed as guards. These guards were not allowed to sit or lie or lean against walls and they could usually be identified because they were the only ones in full uniform and carrying weapons. Now spot the on-duty guard in this photo.

II Wilhelmshaven, III Swinemünde, IV Cuxhaven, V Pillau, VI Emden and VII Memel. The odd numbers were allocated to the Baltic Command and the even numbers to the North Sea. This slowly developing programme did not receive any significant boost until after the start of the War when at least another twenty-five new detachments were added between 1939 and 1941. 1942 was very much a calm year for naval artillery, although a large number of bunkers were still being built. The speed at which this was being done was indeed most remarkable and in many cases it made a most positive contribution to the war effort by releasing ships for other duties. For example, the French-German armistice was signed at the end of June 1940 and the first phase of gun batteries along Pas de Calais were operational in less than three months; they dominated the Straight of Dover to such an extent that part of South East England became known as Hell Fire Corner.

The beginning of the War also saw the introduction of several specialist subdivisions with the naval artillery branch. This included establishing a few –not more than about a dozen – Light Naval Artillery Units (Leichte Marineartillerieabteilungen), many with portable rather than static equipment. Each of the initial seven naval artillery detachments listed above also had a Naval Flak Division (Marineflakeinheit) and these were also enlarged both in size of each group and in number of guns. There were numerous reorganisation programmes resulting in name changes, making it difficult to trace the history of individual units. In September 1940 some of the established anti-aircraft units became known as Naval Onboard Flak Units (Marinebordflakeinheiten). By the end of 1942 the Naval Anti-Aircraft Units alone had a strength of almost 7,000 men, meaning they had become a significant part of the coastal defences and, in some cases, also inland defences.

THE MAIN GERMAN COASTAL BATTERIES OF THE ATLANTIC WALL (WITH 88-MM GUNS OR BIGGER CALIBRES)

The guns and batteries listed below are all functioning ones with proper steel guns capable of shooting. Wooden dummy batteries have not been included.

a. Country

b. Total Number of Batteries

c. Total Number of Guns

d. Naval Gun Batteries

e. Flak Batteries

f. Torpedo Batteries

g. Army and Luftwaffe Batteries

a.	*b.*	*c.*	*d.*	*e.*	*f.*	*g.*
Norway	380	1,437	99	24	15	242
Denmark	48	250	20	10	0	18
German North Sea	55	188	24	31	0	0
Holland	74	289	36	25	0	13
Belgium*	17	75	6	0	0	11
France – Channel	142	562	44	12	0	86
France – Biscay	73	132	30	21	0	22

* The Belgian coast was too small for the Germans to create a separate command and there was some overlap of the Dutch and French Coastal Defence Areas.

The incredible bunker-building programme came to a juddering halt early in 1944 when Field Marshal Erwin Rommel took command of the defences along the French coast. Instead of building more bunkers, the emphasis was switched to fortifying possible landing beaches by adding obstacles in the form of anti-tank cum landing-craft barriers. One of the most common varieties was the Hedgehog, made up of three angular iron girders, joined in the middle to form a three-dimensional cross and often anchored in concrete foundations. Some were laced with explosives set to go off when moved. There was also a tetrahedron, made up of reinforced concrete beams, which could be screwed together to form an anti-tank barrier, and a number of other types. These were supposed

Some bunkers stood out like massive eyesores, while others were camouflaged and dazzle paint was used to hide some of the main features. In this case a doorway has been painted on the back wall. (*Photo: Walter Pätzold and Ariane Krause*)

to have been incredibly effective, easy to build and capable of stopping tanks as well as landing craft, but not the Allied invasion on D-Day. The weak link in this system was that they worked exceedingly well when submerged in water, but the Allies made a point of landing at low tide and could therefore move around the obstacles to avoid detonating them. There is a wonderful collection of many different types of barriers in the Atlantic Wall Museum of Domein Raversijde in Ostend (Belgium).

Although 80 per cent of the Atlantic Wall was built exceedingly quickly, there were considerable problems with the establishment of this long chain of defences. First, the navy did not have the trained personnel to man all the sites and therefore the army provided the manpower for a high proportion of the coastal batteries in foreign countries. This worked reasonably well until the summer of 1941 when German Military Intelligence discovered a massive build-up of Russian weapons poised to head west. The non-aggression pact, signed by Russia and Germany in August 1939 resulted in even the radio monitoring services being prohibited from listening to Russian military radios. Consequently this mass of firepower pointing west came as an unexpected shock and Germany felt there was no alternative other than nip the offensive in the bud, before it could strike. The consequent unexpected attack against the Soviet Union hit the army especially hard and later made it necessary to withdraw troops dug in along part of the Atlantic Wall. This resulted in many batteries being desperately short of manpower.

Naval Infantry

The German Navy had two basic types of uniforms: blue and field grey. Field grey has been translated into English as Naval Infantry, probably because it looks like an infantry rather than a sailors' uniform. However the Reichsmarine of the Weimar Republic and Hitler's Kriegsmarine did not have any long-term infantry divisions. The few divisions remaining from the Kaiser's era were dissolved and never re-established. Naval infantry as such vanished as early as 1872, when it was decided that ships should no longer carry special groups of soldiers and that the ship's crew should deal with all duties, such as landings, guarding the ship and keeping possible unruly sailors under control.

The Kriegsmarine did create some special naval infantry units during the invasion of Norway, mainly to help with the bitter fighting around Narvik. However, these lasted only for a few weeks and were not re-formed until the summer of 1942, when the army had to withdraw soldiers from the Atlantic Wall to help with Operation Barbarossa, the invasion of the Soviet Union. The gaps these withdrawn soldiers left behind were partly filled by men who had never been aboard ships and were sometimes referred to as having been part of the naval infantry, yet technically they wore field grey uniforms and were part of the naval artillery.

Naval infantry units had been split as early as 1849 so that the majority could form what was then called the Naval Corps or the Sea Battalions and a small proportion concentrated on dealing with new recruits. This breaking in of new recruits was developed into an important part of the naval training process. Both the new recruits and their leaders often wore field grey uniforms, but the staff did not come from a land-based part of the navy. They were specially selected sailors from ships and it was considered an honour to be detailed to help with such training.

True naval infantry units were established shortly before the end of the Second World War, mainly in the eastern provinces, to help with the defences against the advancing Red Army. The first of these groups came into being during November 1944 and half a dozen or more were established by the end of March 1945. Their duties included the digging of trenches and fighting on land, but they were poorly equipped, not trained for such tasks and consequently had an incredibly high casualty rate. So much so, that some commanders refused to lay up their ships to form naval infantry units.

The Anatomy of Coastal Artillery Batteries

The majority of military installations in Germany were destroyed shortly after the War and all that remains are a few air raid shelters, which were too difficult to break. It seems likely that the majority of coastal defence installations, with the exception of a few isolated small bunkers have been removed or buried under natural vegetation. Despite this frenzied programme of senseless destruction by the armies of occupation, neither the British nor the American authorities had much influence in Norway, Denmark, Holland, Belgium and France, where a multitude of fortifications still remain in reasonable

Both the army and the navy installed heavy artillery in vulnerable places. Army guns like this one tended to have been modern weapons while the navy used a number of obsolete gun turrets from old ships.

condition. Some bunkers have been demolished, but the majority were either left or handed to the owner of the land on which they stood after dangerous ammunition had been removed. Some were sold together with the land on which they stood. As a result, a good number of excellent museums have grown up in those countries to preserve and re-construct some of the Second World War defences. Making contact with these places of interest is relatively easy these days by using the Internet.

Some bunkers were planned especially for where they are standing (Sonderbunker – Special Bunkers), but the vast majority are of a standard basic design, known as Regelbunker (Standard Bunker) and with a number after the name to identify the particular type. This standardisation made it easy and fast to build because vital dimensions were given and each plan included a shopping list of materials required. Thus fairly inexperienced builders could put them up in the shortest possible time. Either an army or a naval construction department would have supplied the specialist materials for whatever bunker type was being built. This book is too small to include a detailed portrait of the different bunker types and the following is merely a list of the main features to look for when exploring old sites.

Above and right: A vast variety of heavy anti-aircraft guns were installed in naval flak batteries.

A large number of guns in foreign naval coastal batteries had been captured when Germany invaded. Some these had been destroyed beyond use but a large number were only damaged and could be repaired to be used again. Hiding them from view and protecting them from the natural elements was one of the major time-consuming occupations for their crews.

Gun positions

There were three basic types of gun bunkers in addition to anti-aircraft guns, which were often open to the sky without a covering roof. Armoured gun turrets, usually removed from old warships, sat directly on top of strong concrete foundations while guns without their own protection were placed under a thick concrete roof. Large gun turrets on ships were deeper than the armoured structure that rotated above the deck. The ammunition raising and loading mechanism below the turret fitted into an armoured tube leading down to the magazine. This heavy structure, comprised of the gun with the ammunition raising section below it, was simply lowered into the hole and very often rested there on a circular rail without being attached to the ship. When such turrets were embedded on land they sat on top of a ring in raised concrete foundations or the concrete bed had to extend into a hole dug in the ground. The other gun type was held firmly on the floor by a large number of heavy screws embedded in the foundations. The third variety consisted of artillery pieces with wheels for towing behind a tractor or lorry. These were often supplied with special rotating platforms so that the heavy gun could be turned only a fraction at a time to make aiming at moving ships easier than when having to turn a gun mounted on wheels.

Once aircraft were close enough, powerful searchlights were used to find them in the night sky for the anti-aircraft guns.

Arsenals, Magazines and Ammunition Stores

The mass media seems to have forgotten that ammunition is terribly heavy and film heroes toss it around as if it was made from foam rubber. The author can manage to carry one 88-mm or 105-mm cartridge at a time. It is possible that a healthy, younger man might manage two, but there is no way that any individual could manage a box of half a dozen. Therefore, either an overhead gantry system or a trolley system had to be provided for rapidly shooting weapons; heavy guns needed a special system for carrying ammunition from storage areas to the loading mechanism. Cartridges were generally stored inside air and watertight containers that were so efficient that when one finds them today, after more than half a century under water, the shells inside are still shiny. It would appear that waxed cardboard was also used to wrap cartridges. Ammunition for smaller calibre guns was stored inside boxes in such quantities that one or two men could carry one box.

Generally, ammunition for guns up to 105 mm came as standard cartridges with the shell attached. Ammunition for bigger calibres tended to have come in three parts: shells, detonators to fit insider them and propelling explosives.

There were no hard and fast rules about the storage of explosives and fuels other than they should inflict the minimum of damage if accidentally detonated or ignited. A large magazine, often with main line or narrow-gauge rail connections, was usually situated some distance from vital installations. These could range from simple bunkers for holding

There was a considerable shortage of weapons, especially in some of the isolated locations, and everything was brought into service, even old museum pieces. The big problem was moving the heavy artillery to positions where it could be used.

explosives or larger buildings to also accommodate mines and torpedoes. Each battery was usually equipped with facilities to store its own ready-to-use ammunition. Larger guns often had two rooms: one for storing the shells and the other to hold explosives for propelling them. In the olden days the underground rooms had a gap between the interior and the outside wall so that any water seeping in could be drained without making the powder store damp. This principle also applied to many installations from the Second World War, despite explosives being delivered in water and airtight containers.

Brass cartridge cases became quite a problem after they had fired, especially in anti-aircraft sites where several hundred might be shot before there was time to clear the empties away. To overcome this the battery could well have had a pit for dumping used shells so that they could be collected after the battle and sent for recycling.

Control Facilities

The battery commander could well have been a warrant officer or even petty officer, but generally larger sites would have had a core of officers for the main control functions. These men would have been responsible for the efficient running of the battery. In the event of an attack they determined which targets to aim at and gave the order to shoot. This main control centre was often located some distance from the guns to be away from the smoke they caused. In addition to having a main observation and lookout post,

Right and below: The navy had a variety of small-calibre anti-aircraft guns, many of them highly portable, but they required firm foundations if they were going to be effective against fast-flying aircraft. Light flak weapons were often located close to likely targets and their crews suffered an incredibly high casualty rate with many being killed once bombs started falling.

Detecting an approaching enemy in good time to engage it was vital and Germany relied heavily on massive sound detectors similar to ear trumpets to listen for aircraft. Some of them worked electrically with microphones, but the majority were nothing more than a hollow tube connected to the operator's ears to function in a similar way to a doctor's stethoscope. These worked especially well in isolated locations and often gave more accurate information about aircraft flying over clouds than could be obtained by the naked ear.

there could well have been two or more types of control within the system. First, the commanding officer would determine which targets to engage with which guns, then at least one huge optical direction finder determined the distance to the target and passed the details on to the guns.

At the same time it was necessary to determine the speed and direction of the target. At sea, where ships could fire a salvo of several shots from one turret, it was easier to see where the shells splashed into the water, but even when trying to find the exact range with a single gun, special binoculars would be needed for working out the gap between the splash and the target, so that the next shot might be adjusted to be more accurate. These binoculars looked like a range finder but they only provided excellent three-dimensional views and could not measure distances. Information from optical (and later radar) measuring devices was fed into a complicated calculator to work out the firing details for the guns. Command centres were also connected to other bunker systems both by telephone and underground tunnels. The idea being to keep other stations informed of what was going on. As far as possible cables were laid to carry both telephone and telex lines, and the majority of batteries also had their own secure radio rooms with the famous Enigma machines.

Several bunkers in military complexes were sold to private individuals after the War; there were cases where the copper wires removed from the bunker fetched a higher sum on the scrap market than the price paid for the building. Some bunkers had the most sophisticated communication systems with masses of cables almost forming part of the protection.

A Würzburg Riese (Würzburg Giant) radar scanner. The whole contraption rotated and the parabolic aerial tilted so that it could be pointed in any direction. The operators sat in the cabin attached to the rear. Some of these devices were bolted to the ground while others were mounted on railway wagons. Before the War German research into radar had progressed far beyond anything produced by other countries, but most of this was abandoned in 1939 and it was not long before Germany lagged behind in this important field of radiolocation. Yet, research gained a new impetus later during the War and a number of different devices were produced.

Entrances, Air Ducts and Airlocks

Doors, often as small as possible, were usually well armoured with blast protection walls in front of them on the outside or inside. There were a vast variety of doors made by a number of manufacturers. At one end of the spectrum was a simple steel plate, hinged on one side and with a locking mechanism on the other. These were usually fitted as an extra layer on top of the windows and closed only in emergencies. Some were plain steel while others had a soft attachment around the outside to make an airtight seal with the window frame when they were closed. Such shutters were placed on both the outside or on the inside of windows and doors. At the more complicated end of this spectrum were special blast and gas proof doors, often with four or six fastening points operated by a single lever or wheel, similar to pressure resisting doors on ships. These were capable of withstanding heavy blasts.

The threat of gas attacks was a major factor in planning and design; many bunkers were fitted with special protection. Poisonous gasses used during the First World War were heavier than air and tended to flow, like water, into the lowest cavities. Therefore many bunkers were fitted with high chimney-like air intakes and with their own ventilation system. Once this was switched to closed circuit, air would be pumped through a filter containing sodium hydroxide for absorbing carbon dioxide and then through pipes into the extremities of the building. Obviously there were adequate holes in the walls to allow the air to return to the main ventilation pump. Each man would also have had his own gas mask or personal closed-circuit breathing systems. Even bunkers with huge openings for guns often had their own ventilation system to prevent obnoxious gasses from exploding shells interfering with the efficiency of the gun crew. Some bunkers could be sealed off completely against gas attacks and might have had an airlock in addition to the main door or a set of two doors (one behind the other) so that they could be used as an air lock if necessary.

Close Combat Defences

The excellent protection built into bunkers muffled outside sounds, smoke often obscured vision and the lack of windows made it difficult to be fully aware of what was happening around the outside of the bunker. It would have been too easy to approach bunkers from behind and lob hand grenades through gun slits. To prevent such incursions, bunker systems were provided with special close combat facilities, very much in the same vein as medieval archery slots in castle walls or deep holes above doors for pouring down hot liquids. In addition to such shooting holes, bunkers were surrounded by a system of trenches, enabling men to move around the outside and pass from one bunker to another without being seen by an enemy. This trench system was usually defended by a series of barbed wire entanglements, reminiscent of the First World War trench defences, and was often laced with a multitude of anti-personnel mines. These trenches varied from open-top channels with wooden sides to sophisticated brick-lined tunnels with sniper exits. These special machine-gun holes were embedded with an iron ring so that a light to medium-sized weapon, carried by the gunner along the tunnel, could be hooked firmly in place and easily rotated.

The Standby Room

Gun openings were often large enough to emit rain and fine wind-blown sand, which was especially destructive. This mixture acted like sandpaper to form the most incredible jamming paste when mixed with oil or grease. In addition to this, some builders didn't judge the tides terribly well so that seawater also sloshed about in the gun pits. This meant that the gun crews would find themselves in such hostile environments that the natural elements could render their weapons useless. In view of this bunkers were often built with a sealed stand-by room where small weapons, gas masks and ammunition could be stored to be ready for instant use. There were even strict rules and written regulations about how and where items had to be stored in such rooms. These were not always universal, but the men of the same detachment were expected to arrange things the way laid down in the written regulations. The reason for this was not to comply with German tidiness, but to ensure that men moving from one bunker to another did not have to waste time looking for essential items. The same applied to vehicles, where written regulations stated where individual equipment had to be loaded. This meant there were no hitches when men moved from one location to another.

Engine Rooms, Heaters, Air Conditioning and Water

Bunkers tend to remain relatively cool during hot summer sunshine, but they could get excruciatingly cold in winter, especially in the northern latitudes. Lighting was also a problem as that there were hardly any windows and lamps had to remain on all day long. Electrical heaters were still somewhat in their infancy, even if the bunker system could be connected to the outside grid. In any case this was likely to give out at crucial moments and an emergency generator was more than essential. These then had their own fuel tank – either coal or oil. Emergency systems tended to run on oil because it was quicker to start them, but coal was favoured in systems that ran all the time because there was a general shortage of liquid fuels.

In addition to a lighting and heating system, some bunkers were also equipped with air-conditioning to deal with gas attacks. It is quite likely that some bunkers had to tap into a power supply with a higher voltage than the average lighting system could cope with. Therefore some had their own transformers. Water for washing, drinking and fire fighting was also a problem in some parts, especially in the dry sand dunes of the North Sea coasts; therefore it was not unusual to have a tank system within the bunker complex.

Domestic Arrangements

Isolated bunkers could well have been equipped with their own kitchens, recreation areas and sleeping quarters while large sites could well have shared the domestic facilities. Accommodation varied considerably from bunk beds in the corners of some general-purpose room or even in the gunroom, to semi-luxurious hotel-like accommodation. However, all of this was usually so cramped and packed with so much gear that there was hardly room to move about. Some of these bunkers felt a bit like being in a stationary U-boat, with no personal space at all. There appear to have been no hard and fast rules

Many of the guns were hidden in places where they would be most effective and least expected by an intruder, but they hardly ever saw any action. In fact some guns remained hidden in isolated locations throughout the whole War and never fired a shot in anger.

about sleeping while on duty and many of the bigger batteries allowed the duty crew to sleep close to the guns. Anti-aircraft guns varied as well and in some places men stood by ready for action while in others men were allowed to stand down as long as they remained close to their duty positions.

Lavatories varied from flush systems feeding into cesspits to little rooms with buckets, which had to be emptied when full. The throwaway society of modern times had not yet established itself during the War, and such sites did not generate a great deal of trash. It was common to pay a deposit on bottles and return them after use and even empty tins were collected to be used more than once by cutting off the old top to re-sharpen the sides and then resealing it with a new lid and another load of food inside. During the War and shortly after it, there were numerous small businesses specialising in the re-sealing of tins. Anyone with a small garden could bring their own home-grown vegetables in the tins and have them sealed again. It is unlikely that the majority of bunkers would have had a dustbin collection and much of the rubbish was buried in pits or dumped in a convenient shell hole. As late as the 1990s several quarries digging out sand and shingle passed it along a conveyor belt with a massive electro magnet over the top to pull out any iron from the Second World War. This was then dumped into a nearby hole especially dug for the purpose.

Although considerable effort went into clearing mines after the War, it is surprising how much ready-to-use ammunition still turns up these days because it had been left somewhere, simply forgotten, and then buried by the natural elements. Some of the hardware in these bunkers was difficult to get out and then too expensive to be removed by scrap merchants, so many bits and pieces remained in situ. There were many cases where German soldiers walked away from their bunkers at the end of the War, taking with them only their personal possessions and leaving the military equipment where it was. Doors were quickly hidden by rubble thrown up from explosions or wind-blown sand buried the only entrance.

Fort Kugelbake in Cuxhaven

Kugelbake is the name of a huge wooden marker on the first piece of land as one approaches the Elbe Estuary from the sea. Modern navigation aids and other high buildings make this relic from the past superfluous today, but it is still maintained as an ancient symbol of Cuxhaven.

The war against Denmark in 1850, when Wilhelm Bauer built Germany's first submarine, the Brandtaucher, spurred Prussia into a cohered plan for building all manner of frontier and coastal fortifications. The following years also saw significant technical developments with the production of artillery. Better steel and new manufacturing techniques made it possible to produce larger calibres and to increase their effective range and accuracy. Unlike Britain, Germany did not go through the Martello Tower stage; instead of spending vast sums on cementing bricks together to make thick walls for holding a single gun, the German defences were often nothing more than elaborate pits, with the gun shooting over the top of a low earthen bank. While such gun pits continued to be built, the German

The Naval Battery Oldenburg by the side of the Calais ferry terminal, photographed in 2011. The bunkers here are enormous and pictures like this hardly give any indication of massive size.

One of big gun ports at the Naval Battery Oldenburg in Calais with a person to give some idea of scale.

military also embarked upon a more technical approach and considerable resources were devoted to the study of military fortifications. As a result the simple gun pits gave way to massive and highly complicated forts with a multitude of defences.

The foundation stones for a number of forts guarding deep-water channels along the North Sea coasts were laid shortly before France declared war on Prussia in 1870. The French had hoped that the German Catholic states of the south would help suppress the protestant economic uprising in the north, but this did not happen. Instead a combined German army occupied France, surrounded Paris and then, in 1871, declared themselves to be one unified nation with the King of Prussia as Emperor. This meant that France was left not only to nurse heavy wounds but was also forced to pay considerable war reparations. This relieved the German taxpayer of funding the expensive new fortifications and, of course, the majority of ordinary Germans supported the government's new protection programme. Thus hurriedly constructed gun pits could be replaced by the state-of-the-art fortifications.

The forts guarding the deep-water shipping channels of the North Sea took on a considerably more important role in 1911, when the Kiel Canal was inaugurated. Interestingly enough, seven years later, at the end of the First World War, France was instrumental in determining that many of these oppressive forts be removed or at least demilitarized. As a result the majority have disappeared. Forts in sought-after areas have been demolished and the land redeveloped, but quite a few in more isolated positions remained to be re-colonized by nature. The only remaining North Sea fort in Germany is Fort Kugelbake in Cuxhaven. This should also have been abandoned after the First World War as well, but being well away from houses the fort had its guns dismantled but its moat and walls remained as a safe location for storing old unwanted ammunition.

Being in a prime position Fort Kugelbake was partly re-used when the Second World War started. After that war there was such a dire shortage of accommodation that over twenty families made it their home before the site was finally abandoned. In 1992 it was recognized as an important part of history and classified as a Listed Building. Since then it has been restored and can be visited, although it is necessary to join a guided group and the opening times are somewhat limited.

Fort Kugelbake was one of the largest North Sea defences, consisting of a pentagonal structure, roughly 250 metres along its widest diameter and 150 metres along its shortest. This may have been one of the largest along the North Sea coast, but it was tiny when compared with British coastal forts of the period. One of the redoubts in the moat of the fort on Dover's Western Heights, for example, covers a considerably bigger area and is several floors high. German inland fortifications, such as the fortress at Ehrenbreitstein, guarding the Mosel Estuary on the Rhine at Koblenz, are considerably bigger and have far more cunning features than the comparatively simple Fort Kugelbake.

The main core housed a number of large-calibre guns surrounded by a mound and wall dropping into an impressive moat. When it was built, the whole area was a low sandbank with very little vegetation and any hole dug in the ground was likely to fill immediately with water, thus it is no wonder that the landward sides were surrounded by a moat. Periodic high tides flooded the area until the dyke, which now protects it from the tides

Right: The entrance for the medical bunker at the Naval Battery Oldenburg in Calais. One wonders whether the red crosses on the walls were original or whether graffiti artists added them.

Below: Part of the bunker system at Ijmuiden in Holland in 2011, showing a tiny fraction of what is still remaining from the last war. Parts of this complex are now being made into a museum.

A common, multi-purpose, medium to large-calibre gun of the type found in a number of coastal batteries in Germany. The armoured roofs were often not capable of withstanding a direct hit, but they proved to be more than adequate for protecting the crew and the delicate parts of the gun from flying splinters thrown up by near misses. This picture was taken at Fort Kugelbarke in Cuxhaven.

and cuts the fort off from the river, was added as late as the 1960s. Living conditions in the fort were poor due to the intense dampness and the fort had hardly been completed when the authorities added a set of supporting barracks in the town of Cuxhaven. That meant that only the duty soldiers had to endure the permanent dampness. There was no question of abandoning this soggy location because it occupied the prime position for guarding the deep-water shipping channel leading to the Kiel Canal at Brunsbüttel and to Germany's largest port in Hamburg.

In 1911 Fort Kugelbake was supplied with a new innovation, a massive searchlight with an almost 5-kilometre-long beam, making it probably the most powerful lamp of the period. Neither this nor the large guns of what was supposed to have been the largest coastal fortification of the time were ever put to the test during the First World War. The men were put on high alert for the first wartime Christmas Day when a British airship raided the Zeppelin base a few miles away at Nordholz. There were a few other minor incursions, but no suitable targets came within range of the fort's heavy artillery.

The Second World War hard hardly started when newly installed heavy anti-aircraft guns of 88 mm and 105 mm brought down one of three Wellington bombers seen flying out of the Elbe Estuary. The injured plane lost height and crashed near Elbe 1, the lightship furthest out in the estuary. The date, given in the fort's information board, of 2 September 1939 seems to be a little uncertain because it is unlikely that a group of three British bombers should fly into German airspace one day before the declaration of war on 3 September.

The following month saw considerable activity in the German river estuaries of the North Sea and this vintage site was strengthened with a number of additional coastal gun batteries, many more anti-aircraft sites and all manner of other military facilities. Railways had already made Cuxhaven one of the most important fishing ports with a massive daily turnover, constantly sending fresh fish to many inland destinations. In addition to this, the port was also home to one of the biggest minesweeping groups. As a result the harbour was protected by a mass of guns, capable of dealing with aircraft and surface targets. There were also several searchlight batteries and a mine store. Despite the shallow coastal water making it difficult for deep-draught ships to enter the estuary, a massive anti-submarine net with explosive attachments stretched across the deep water as far as the Schleswig-Holstein coast. Gun batteries with naval crews were provided in profusion and isolated sites were established for several miles along the shores. All of these, except Fort Kugelbake, were removed after the War and now it is exceedingly difficult to find any signs of remnants. In fact there has been so much change that it is even difficult to establish exactly where the military sites have been. Fort Kugelbake was stripped of almost all iron and steel, and the majority of concrete bunkers were also demolished. The remains of the gun battery by the U-boat Museum in Altenbruch can just about be made out from the top of the dyke. It is located in some rough ground a few metres east of the Beach Restaurant. If one looks exceedingly hard, one can just make out the shapes of the circular gun emplacements.

THE FRISIAN ISLAND OF WANGEROOGE

Hans-Jürgen Jürgens published a most astonishing diary of life on the Frisian Islands of Wangerooge, Spiekeroog and Langeoog throughout the war years (see Bibliography). In over 700 pages he describes with many photographs how the War hit these small isolated communities and how they were fortified for the defence of the Reich. The following information has been extracted from his book and from a map drawn by Bruno Albers because it provides interesting details of the fortifications established on the offshore islands.

Defence installations on Wangerooge towards the end of 1944 along the north coast from west to east:

One of the massive gun bunkers at Ijmuiden in Holland, showing that some attempt was made to make the surface look like sand.

The rear of an observation and command bunker at Ijmuiden, showing how wind-blown sand is capable of burying even such large structures as these.

Looking out towards the sea from one of the large gun ports at Ijmuiden. During the War this bunker would have had a brilliant view of the water but wind-blown sand has built up in front and the beach is now some distance beyond these dunes.

The author exploring what was probably one of the domestic bunkers at the Ijmuiden battery.

1. Two radar towers of Type Wassermann
2. Searchlight
3. 4 x 20-mm Flak
4. Freya radar mast 'Fritz'
5. 4 x 20-mm and 37-mm Flak for training
6. 1 x 305-mm gun
7. 4 x 105-mm Flak Battery Saline
8. 6 x small-calibre Flak set up towards the end of the War
9. Searchlight
10. 6 x 20-mm and 37-mm Flak for training
11. 6 x 305-mm guns Battery Friedrich August
12. Searchlight
13. 4 x 280-mm guns Battery Graf Spee
14. 2 x Würzburg Riesen radar masts
15. 1 x Freya radar mast
16. Naval signal station
17. 1 x Würzburg Riese radar mast
18. 1 x 20-mm Flak
19. 6 x 20-mm Flak for training
20. 6 x 150-mm guns of Battery Jade [removed later in the War]
21. Searchlight
22. 1 x Würzburg Riese radar mast
23. 4 x 150-mm guns Battery Jade East
24. 1 x 20-mm Flak
25. 4 x 105-mm Battery Neudeich
26. 1 x 37-mm Flak
27. 1 x 20-mm Flak
28. 2 x 105-mm Battery Ostdüne
29. Searchlight
30. 4 x medium dummy gun battery made from timber and painted grey
31. 1 x 20-mm Flak
32. Searchlight
33. 1 x Würzburg Riese radar mast
34. Searchlight
35. 4 x 88-mm guns for surface targets Battery Strandbake

In addition to this, there were several guns and searchlights around the airfield and several other smaller guns dotted around the island. About one hundred bunkers were built on the island throughout the war.

The heavy screws for holding the gun are still visible in the year 2011 in this Ijmuiden bunker.

The gun pit of one of the Ijmuiden bunkers.

Above and below: Exploring old bunker sites can be most fascinating and it is tempting to venture inside. Great care must be taken because it is easy to get into some, but exceedingly difficult to get out again.

A Naval Gun Battery: Domein Raversijde (Ostend, Belgium), Atlantic Wall Museum

These days it is easy to walk into impressive museums, to be struck by sounds and smells from the past, to be confronted with propaganda that should have been buried shortly after the War and to meet entertaining re-enactors. The Atlantic Wall Museum at Domein Raversijde, close to Ostend Airport in Belgium, is astonishingly different. It doesn't come over as a museum at all. Instead one has the impression of being dropped through a time warp; it feels as though you are trespassing on history the moment it is being made.

The Germans established the gun battery *Aachen* at Domein Raversijde during the First World War and re-occupied the site under the new name of *Saltzwedel* in 1940. It was then rebuilt to the latest specifications. The owner of the land, Prince Charles, Count of Flanders, did not allow the site to be ravaged after the War. As a result there are now three marvellous museums where he lived until his death in 1983. The parts relating to the Atlantic Wall are enormous and at least three hours are required for a simple tour, for which audio guides are available in English. Much has been reconstructed with full-scale

A small-calibre anti-aircraft gun by the side of the road at the Raversijde Atlantic Wall Museum in Ostend (Belgium).

An anti-tank gun waiting for uninvited guests.

waxworks in the concrete installations; there is an abundance of heavy artillery, many bunkers, masses of other exhibits and what seems to be an almost endless network of tunnels. Above all, the site is saturated in atmosphere and the richness and number of the exhibits is astounding. This has been recreated the way Field Marshal Erwin Rommel would have seen it during his first inspection in December 1943.

The Atlantic Wall Museum at Domein Raversijde is one of the few places within easy reach of mainland Britain (a day-trip would suffice) where one can not only see a German gun battery but also experience what it must have been like to live in it. The opening hours are limited and Domein Raversijde lacks the usual moneymaking visitor support attractions found in so many British museums. The cafeteria is a long way away and one would get terribly wet if it happens to rain, but the site itself is far beyond fantastic. Domein Raversijde, Nieuwpoortsesteenweg 636, 8400 Oostende, Belgium. www.west-vlaanderen.be/raversijde

Above and below: A large gun visible from the road running along the beach at the Raversijde Atlantic Wall Museum in Ostend (Belgium).

The first thing one notices at Domein Raversijde is that it lacks clutter. Barriers and directions come over as having been left behind from the War and anyone engrossed in conversation could well walk past some of the fascinating objects without noticing them. This one, the dish of a Würzburg Riese radar aerial, is large enough not to be missed. During the War it would have been standing up, fixed either to a solid concrete mount of attached to a trailer. It had a cabin at the base for operators and there were masses of these along the coasts from north Norway as far as the south of France. A variety of different models existed and caused a great stir in England when they were first spotted. British Commandos mounted a special raid on a radar site at Bruneval in France to capture the important parts of such an instrument.

It is strange that there were so many searchlights during the War, but that so few of them remain and one hardly sees any in action these days. The Germans had a variety of differently sized lamps from about 600 cm in diameter for small-calibre guns to huge 2,000-cm lights. Several men would have been required to operate one of these and special search light units manned them.

Many of the small portable items of defence have vanished and seeing this vast collection of obstacles at Ostend was a real treat. It is weird to think that at one time beaches along the continental coast would have been festooned with an array of such obstacles, some of them attached to explosives, which detonated when moved. These flimsy looking obstacles were made from a minimum of materials and were probably just as effective as the much heavier British 'Dragons' Teeth' that can still be seen in South East England.

Many of the weapons for coastal defences, especially in foreign countries, were a mishmash of what was available; old guns, weapons from decommissioned ships, captured equipment and even items from museums. This is a 75-mm PAK 40 anti-tank gun (Panzer-abwehr-kanone – all one word meaning Tank Defence Cannon) with an effective range of about 8 kilometres. The wires in front of it belong to the coastal tramway and were not there during the War.

A 20-mm Oerlikon was a general-purpose cannon that could be used against aircraft. It had an effective range of almost 4.5 kilometres, but hitting small aircraft at that distance was incredibly difficult. Yet the gun's rapid fire could make a real mess of targets even over such a considerable distance. These guns were modified in various ways for use in specialised locations. They were made under licence and used by both sides throughout the War. The name Oerlikon was derived from a suburb of Zürich in Switzerland where the initial manufacturer had his first headquarters.

A 120-mm quick-firing gun made in 1931 by Cockerill of Liege (Belgium) with an effective range of about 17.5 kilometres. Although most impressive, the vast majority of these large guns never fired a shot in anger throughout the entire War. In this case it looks as if the gun has been placed into a pit designed for some other weapon.

A 37-mm PAK (Panzer-abwehr-kanone – all one word meaning Tank Defence Cannon) anti-tank gun with a range of 6.8 kilometres. Hitting a tank at such vast distances was more than difficult, even when it was moving straight towards the gun. Yet these comparatively light weapons (450 kilograms) were most effective because they could be moved so easily and they dealt a significant blow against quite heavily armoured vehicles over considerable distances.

40-mm Flak 28 Bofors gun with a range of about almost 9 kilometres. Bofors was a Swedish firm that developed and built medium sized anti-aircraft guns for the navy and these were later produced under licence by both sides of the Second World War, although they were heavily modified and many had a variety of different sights attached to them.

A general-purpose 20-mm German Mauser built in 1938. The Mauser was originally designed to cope with aircraft and had a range of just over 2 kilometres. It had a rapid rate of fire, but was not the easiest to handle and was not generally adopted by the navy, which preferred weapons that were easier to aim and operate against fast flying aircraft.

Opposite above and below: Looking at coastal defences one comes across two main types of bunkers. Ones that were purpose-built around a specific gun or others with huge, well-armoured doors at the back to accommodate a variety of weapons. One has to be impressed by the lengths to which the designers went for protecting both guns and their crews. Although these bunkers look spacious when visiting them these days, it must be remembered that a good number of people would have been required to fire the gun and ready-to-use ammunition would have been stored inside the bunker as well.

Left: A 37-mm anti-aircraft gun with a range of about 14 kilometres, built around 1936. This was a semi-automatic version that was improved throughout the War and differed considerably from the same calibre deck guns fitted to ships and U-boats. The deck guns were intended for surface targets and shells had to be fed singly into the breech. This anti-aircraft version put up a good rate of fire, but those fitted to small ships were not accurate enough for coping with modern fast-flying aircraft with armour at the front of the vital components.

Below: Trinkwasser – Drinking Water – was probably one of the most important provisions for a vast number of coastal defence installations from Calais to as far as the north of Denmark. Much of this coast consists of vast sand dunes where wind-blown particles can form an annoying intrusion on the best of days and there was no water in those arid, desert-like areas. Pipes would have supplied bunkers near towns, but many men had to rely on tanks like this.

This page and next page above: Although open trenches with wooden, corrugated iron or brick sides were common along the continental coasts, at Domein Raversijde there was also a vast network of totally enclosed tunnels. These had holes along them at regular intervals so that men could appear at strategic points among the high marram grass for shooting at an invading enemy. The ground around defensive installations was usually laced with a variety of barbed wire entanglements, making it difficult for invaders to run or even lie down to hide. Each of these shooting holes was fitted with a circular metallic rail for holding the special bi-pod legs of a machine gun. They were quite deadly because the gunners would have been difficult to spot and they were in a good position to obtain an accurate aim. Wind-blown sand-jamming guns made it impractical to fix small weapons in place and gun crews would have carried their weapons and ammunition to wherever they were directed.

A recreation of a First World War installation with men from the Naval Artillery Division.

Above and below: A depiction of a First World War scene in a communications bunker brought to life not only with what would have been there but also with items soldiers would have left lying about during their daily duties. The white, circular objects on the wall are covers for electrical fuses and the men had an oil lamp for when power failures were beyond their control.

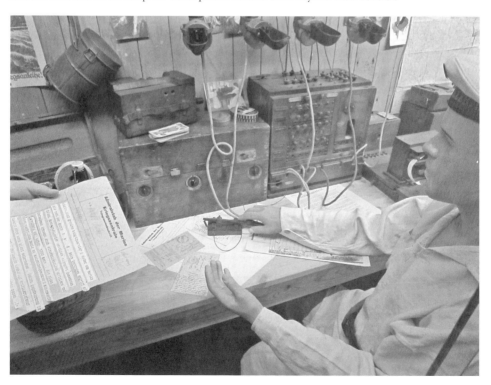

The vast majority of bunkers during both World Wars would not have been in such isolated positions that they were not connected to the mains telephone net and only the command post would have had external communications. Yet, communications within each defensive site would have been vital and intercom telephones were installed in large numbers. These were very often powered by only a small battery and connected by a single wire. A conductor driven into the earth then served as second link to make the connection. Such systems worked exceedingly well except that they didn't have enough power to operate a bell because that required more electricity. Therefore each set had a dynamo inside and turning the handle on the side of the telephone rang the bells. The notice on the front says: Attention the enemy is listening in – ring off three times after each conversation.

Any military installation set up for a commanding officer's inspection would look rather bland in a museum and it is easy to assume that these displays showing the life inside the bunkers have had too much clobber added. This may be partly true, but men who served in these places said that space was exceedingly cramped and often there was hardly room to move about. Some of the front line bunkers were so tight that men even operated a hot bunking system while on duty there. This meant a man coming off duty would occupy a bunk vacated by a man going out to take his place. Obviously the spaces where large guns were mounted had to be considerably bigger to allow for movement of the weapon and the gasses and pressures that emanated from it.

Opposite page: Living space often had to double up as workspace and many coastal installations had to make maximum use of the available space. It is obviously pay day here with a non-commissioned administration officer handing out money and selling stamps. Stamps are rather curious because there seems to have been no hard and fast rules about who could use the free Feldpost (Field Post) system. Even some front line troops stationed abroad had to buy stamps. As far as possible men stationed in bunkers were supplied with their own bed and a lockable cupboard. These cupboards tended to have been all of similar design, especially made to accommodate military uniforms and there were strict rules about how and where things had to be stored inside it.

Left and below: Engineering workshops were a vital part of any defensive system. The throwaway life that we live in today hadn't yet come of age during the Second World War and there was no way that any military gear could be jettisoned if it was still repairable. Even land-based units had to economise with their hardware.

Opposite above: As on ships, every available space was used and even corridors doubled up as living areas. On the right are standard military lockers and the four padlocks suggest four men used these four cupboards. Generally the navy was a little more generous with space and provided a slightly wider, double-fronted cupboard for each man.

Oposite below: A bunkroom with a total of fifteen beds. Imagine this tiny space when all of the men have to get ready for a parade or inspection. The cylinders above the helmets on the far wall contained gas masks. The boards that appear to be lying on the floor are the top of a table.

Above: Officers, both commissioned and warrant officers, were usually provided with superior accommodation to the men, although they too lived and worked in exceedingly tight spaces. The majority of dogs were not there for cuddling but to help men patrolling the extensive grounds around military installations. In addition to obvious attacks from the sea or from paratroopers dropped inland, the guards always had to be on the lookout for saboteurs and local burglars.

Left: This shows an interesting combination of uniforms and an even more fascinating Enigma coding machine. Ships at sea used a more sophisticated machine with a plug board in the front to make decoding considerably more difficult. The Konteradmiral (Rear Admiral) on the right had the standard gold braid on his uniform while the silver braid of the Leutnant zur See (Junior Lieutenant) on the left indicates that he is an administration officer. The man at the back is wearing the field grey naval uniform for men based on land.

One has to bear in mind that ten years after the end of the War there were still houses in London without electricity. These were usually lit by gas. Similar conditions prevailed on the continent and many military installations were far enough away from settlements not have been near an electrical supply. Even those installations close to housing found that the power was sometimes rationed to specific periods or it was cut off without warning. Some coastal defences had their own power supply while others had emergency generators, which were turned on when the main power failed. This was more than essential inside a large network of rooms and tunnels without windows and often with only very tiny doors.

Above and left: The quartermaster's stores formed an important part of all military bases and one wonders what was stored in all the boxes and how anyone ever worked out where wanted items were located. As far as possible the military tried to transport goods in such a manner that observers could not derive too much information from what they were seeing. For that reason boxes were usually disguised and instead of descriptive names they had code numbers on the outside to identify the contents.

Above: Nothing could destroy morale quicker than poor food. The food supplied to land-based units was often not as diverse as that given to sailors aboard ships and men in coastal defences had to put up with monotonous diets, but despite all these wartime limitations, the quartermaster's larder was still a most important part of any defensive operation. Considerable quantities of preserved food had to be stored because deliveries were not only irregular but they could not always be guaranteed.

Right: The blackboard outside the kitchen states that on 11 May 1943 the menu was:
Lunch – Soup, roast beef and potatoes.
Evening meal – Liver sausage, dripping, half a loaf of bread and five cigarettes.

Above and below: Marine-Küsten-Polizei (Naval Coast Police). The armband on the left sleeve of the standing man states Marineküstenpolizei and the same is written on the metal plate he is wearing around the neck. This plate indicates that he is on duty. As with all naval greatcoats, there are no rank markings on the sleeve and the only indication of rank are the shoulder lapels. The gold braid with the two pips indicates he is a warrant officer.

Above and below: Despite going on duty during unsociable hours and having to put up with appalling conditions, daily routines had to continue and personal grooming and darning one's uniform formed a major part of the off-duty periods, even within the tight confines of bunker life.

Above: Although many of the coastal batteries never fired a shot in anger throughout the entire War, there were still injuries and illnesses to deal with. Just look at any business to see how many employees have to take time off each month for medical reasons. The military medical service was not just there to patch up men injured in action, they also had to see to the well-being of those who fell ill or were injured during the course of their duties.

Left: This notice saying that damage to communication and radio equipment will be punished would suggest that not everybody in the base was in harmony with Germany's war effort.

CHAPTER 11
Naval Fire Fighters

Much of this chapter is based on files in the German U-boat Museum compiled by Ernst Mecke, who established the first naval fighting unit in Kiel, and on information from Hans Brunswig, author and fire chief from Hamburg.

British forces confiscated many German fire-fighting records, including veterinary accounts of the Second World War and it looks as if most of them have been deliberately destroyed to hide the evidence of their massive bombing campaign. The ferocious bombing of British cities by the Luftwaffe is very well documented, and rightly so, but the Museum for Hamburg History was not allowed to keep records or display exhibits focusing on the devastating bombing offensive by the Allied air forces. As a result very little has been written about the fire fighters of the Second World War, although many of them contributed more than some highly decorated soldiers. Many firemen were constantly faced with the harsh reality of death in its cruellest and most inhuman form, putting immense emotional and physical strain on them. Just reading or hearing about their exploits makes one feel sick and one wonders how they coped with the harsh punishment of doing their duty.

The amazing beginning of the German Naval Fire Service shows how propaganda and obedience can influence the highest ranking and most powerful officials. Before the War Reichsmarschall Hermann Göring boasted that it would be impossible for hostile aircraft to fly over Germany; as a result his Luftwaffe was developed without regard to any form of civil defence. Discussing possible air raid precautions or making plans for building air raid shelters was considered to have been subversive. Even the navy, with huge bases offering incredibly easy fixed targets for bombers, did not make any significant air defence plans until after the start of the War. To make the situation worse, once the War had begun, highly specialised fire fighters were called up for national service and others who volunteered ended up working in military offices, doing the type of jobs that could have been done by anyone without their distinctive qualifications and experience. Luckily for the Germans, initial British bomb aiming was pretty pathetic and the Royal Air Force tended to concentrate on soft targets, rather than essential military installations. During the famous Battle of Britain, for example, the Royal Air Force provoked Germany into attacking by focusing especially on children. Colourful cards, attractive to youngsters and containing phosphorous wrapped in damp cloth, were dropped over cities. Once

The remains of a fire engine in Hamburg. Streets were often littered with so much debris that vehicles could no longer pass along them and at times blockaded even heavy vehicles into an inferno. Men managed to escape on foot, but they still had an incredibly high casualty rate. (*Photo: Hans Brunswig*)

in children's pockets the cards burst into flames to cause the most horrific injuries. In addition to this, Hans Brunswig spoke of an incident where several isolated hospitals and convalescent homes along the North Sea coast were apparently singled out for attack.

Raids like these provided the impetus and determination for the navy to establish its own Fire Fighting Service. The first division was set up in Kiel under the leadership of Ernst Mecke and became quite an eye opener for the military rigidity; making it necessary for higher officials to adjust their thinking rather quickly. Instead of joining the queue and asking the high admirals where they might be accommodated, the men from new Fire Service chose the best locations themselves, informed the admiral where the bases were going to be and literally started building their own headquarters. These buildings might have consisted of well-insulated huts whose wood had been treated with fire-retarding chemicals, but they were put up in exactly the right locations to reach any part of the base. Luckily a high proportion of the recruits had come from the naval reserve and had brought with them the expertise to carry out all aspects of this exacting construction work. It was no easy task and involved much more planning than erecting a few wooden buildings on piles of bricks. Good access roads were essential; the men and their cumbersome equipment needed to reach all vulnerable areas. The huts had to provide more than the usual military accommodation, to cope with a full compliment of on and off-duty staff. Working a pattern of 24 hours on and then 24 hour off, it was still necessary for the off-duty crew to remain in the base because it was foreseen that both sets would be required in an emergency. Such working practice may have been standard aboard ships since time immemorial, but it was radically new for the majority of men joining the fire brigade. In view of this the base had to provide good washing facilities for dealing with clothes as well as for men returning from duty. A cinema plus all the usual recreation areas were needed as well and on top of that training areas, maintenance workshops and equipment storage had to be added. The first Naval Fire Fighting Service in Kiel was made up of 800 men, half of them on the eastern side of the port and the other on the west, but this number was quickly enlarged to several thousand, based in more than just two locations. Such large numbers made it obvious that these new headquarters would have to be vast and could easily be looked upon as a brilliant target for passing aircraft. Therefore they were hidden in parks, among trees and made to look as if they had always been there.

The fact that the planners of this new naval branch had done their work well was later verified when men on active duty hardly ever made use of leave passes and spent their free time within the base rather than joining other sailors in the amusement quarters of town. The naval fire fighting service provided quite far-sighted and large-scale amenities for married men, by renting a large number of comfortable rooms in private flats so that wives and children could come to stay. The overnight accommodation was necessary because many of the men were not locals and had come from far afield. Allowing the families to visit the men was a good deal more practical than sending the men home on holiday.

Existing ideas about fire fighting had to change rapidly once air raids became more frequent. At first members of the fire brigade were ordered to make use of air raid shelters until the all clear sounded. This meant they often arrived at a fire when it had already got a firm hold. Bearing in mind that the majority of people lived in four-storey flats and those on the top usually stored their heating coal in the loft, firemen were often faced with large flames and incredible heat, making it virtually impossible to extinguish the fire. So, the working practice was changed and a number of lookouts were posted on high vantage points to report the compass bearing of any smoke they spotted. The central control room would then plot such positions on a large map and dispatch the nearest fire-fighting unit as soon as the coordinates gave them a definite position. Thus fire engines could set out before the fire gained a serious hold. The obvious disadvantage with this was that both men and equipment would be put at risk and many men and women lost their lives as a result, but it was felt that this would have to become part of a necessary and acceptable risk because the alternative would have resulted in an even higher loss of life and property.

Despite the civil fire brigade being rapidly enlarged and remaining highly active to deal with the majority of fires in town, naval firemen had to learn how to cope with house fires in addition to dealing with incidents inside the hemmed-in confines of ships. The majority of people would have reached air raid shelters before bombs started bursting,

Wooden houses, especially large public buildings such as this railway station suffered enormously from incendiary bombs and often there was little that could be done to save them because fires got a fierce grip before any fire fighting appliances could be brought near to them.

so often there was no need for firemen to venture into burning buildings to save lives. With ships this was totally different and even their sophisticated foam equipment could not always cope with such acute incidents. Venturing into hot, smoke-filled quarters to find the fire started to become part of everyday work. To deal with this, the Naval Fire Service was supplied with superior breathing apparatus, oxyacetylene burners for cutting holes in metal and with other modern aids. Hans Brunswig explained how men cut holes into the sides of fiercely burning fuel tanks, hoping they were well above the level of the liquid, in order to fill the empty space with foam and thus starve the fire of what looked like a vast primus stove.

The first recruits were ordinary soldiers under the leadership of trained fire fighters. Wearing officially grey naval infantry uniforms, their working gear was similar to what other land-based sailors were wearing, but the fire fighters had some special modifications. They can be easily distinguished in photographs by their modified helmets. The backs of these had a large, thick leather skirt, running down to well below the shoulders, making it difficult for anything to fall down the collar. In addition to this, the high leather boots issued to these men had a cavalry type of fastening on the top so that nothing could fall into them. Since rubber would have melted when it got hot, the soles were similar to those worn by mountaineers of the time, made of thick leather and a good lacing of

Although ships were made from iron, it is surprising how well they burned and many smouldered into wrecks of twisted iron merely because fires started in such confined spaces that fire fighters could not get close enough to the flames.

heavy iron studs. Brushing these into a brilliant shine, as was common in the armed services, was not part of the daily routine because wax could burn and turn the protective footwear into an undesirable toaster.

Many fires caused by incendiary bombs started at the top rather than the bottom of buildings and entering these was not always advisable. Staircases were often made of wood and the stairwells could well have been without daylight. In view of this, it was necessary for men to climb up the outside of houses, even when turntable ladders were not available because these were used elsewhere. To do this, they were equipped with a naval belt, modified to a pre-war fire brigade pattern with a huge karabiner and a fastening strong enough to hold the weight of at least two men. A ladder with a large bracket on the top and long enough to reach up one floor would be smashed through a window so that the bracket held it in place as the ladder hung down the outside wall. (Many blocks of flats had balconies, so these were used in preference to smashing windows.) The first man would then climb up one floor so that the second could hand him the next ladder to reach one floor higher until there were ladders hanging up the outside of the house, often reaching up to the loft space above the fourth or fifth floor. Pre-war planning regulations did not allow for buildings higher than five floors because the fire brigades' turntable ladders could not reach any higher.

Left: The fire fighter with a thick leather skirt attached to his helmet is hidden behind this group. It looks as if some youngsters are lending a hand with bringing the injured out of a bombed building.

Below: This extending ladder clearly shows why the fire brigade suffered such enormous casualties with their machinery. Reaching the fire was often easy, but extracting appliances from hot locations was sometimes impossible and all the men could do was to run for their lives. (*Photo: Hans Brunswig*)

Photos like this could have been taken anywhere in wartime Europe and one must wonder at the masses of passers by who stopped to help. Fire fighters were supplied with special hobnail boots, but it looks as if some ordinary person with plain leather soles has clambered into this wrecked building to search for another soul that might still be alive.

Climbing up the outside of a building was relatively quick and often safer than venturing into a burning interior, especially if there were balconies to help the men. Yet handling those ladders involved a good deal of teamwork and skill to prevent the heavy weight from pulling the men off balance. Once at the top, men often abseiled down again, in order to keep to a one-way traffic up the ladders. Just this one simple exercise shows that the men had to develop similar skills to well-trained mountaineers as well as learn how to cope with sophisticated mechanical equipment down on the ground. The problem was that there was often very little time to learn.

Once the Allied air forces intensified their bombing campaign and were obviously aiming their wrath on housing areas, it became obvious that the system of having a rigid base was no longer of much use. At first firemen dashed out a fire and then returned to the headquarters, but now things were becoming so intense that they moved from one operation to another, without time for returning to base in between. So, the plans created at the beginning of the War had to be modified. Mobile support units with shelter, food and drink had to accompany the men into action areas. The average, self-contained unit was made up of several fire engines consisting of powerful pumps with a more than adequate supply of hoses. These would have had at least one revolving extending ladder mounted on a lorry chassis. There would also have been a mobile workshop with generator and crane, a set of accommodation vans for men to rest and to feed during bad weather, at least a couple of medical vans with trained first aiders and a mobile carbon dioxide plant, usually with foam generator attached to it. At the other end of this mobility scale were a number of official cycles. These provided quick transport and could easily be carried when roads were covered with so much bombing rubble that vehicles could not get through.

The problem with the incessant bombing raids was that life had to continue and often there was no alternative to using heavily bombed out locations. Long-distance bus stops were a good example. Buses often still made their way to where the pre-war stops had been, even if it meant penetrating into heavily bombed parts. Surprisingly enough, the drivers found that there were enough passengers getting on and off, even in such desolate areas of almost total destruction.

The Naval Fire Brigade made a point of not accepting officers or middle management leaders from outside establishments. Instead they created their own promotion system and made it possible for a simple sailor to rise rapidly to officer rank. This allowed for an exchange of men from one company to another, but ensured that an experienced individual, whom the men could trust, would be responsible for making the necessary life-threatening instant decisions.

Being a naval fire fighting service meant it was necessary to have some specialised equipment for reaching ships in the harbour, but before the War the navy had not got around to building its own specialised fire fighting vessels. Indeed, there weren't many civilian ones either, meaning it was not possible to instantly commandeer a fleet. Thus the navy set about fitting some powerful pumps to existing ships and at the same time negotiating contracts with private shipbuilders to fill the gap. As a result August Pahl, the biggest of the smaller shipyards on Finkenwerder in Hamburg and close to the huge Deutsche Werft, was appointed to build the navy's first specialised fire fighting vessels. This was by no means an easy task, since plans hardly existed and there was no one around with the necessary experience to build such complicated craft. Yet, twenty or more were instantly required. Kiel and Wilhelmshaven were due to receive three each, Swinemünde and Gotenhafen two each and many of the other ports at least one. August Pahl's shipyard was founded around 1914 and it seems to have vanished from the scene as late as the 1990s. During those years it built a number of flat-bottomed Alsterdampfer (flat-bottomed steamers for operating on the Alster River/Lake) for use in Hamburg, several ferries, lifeboats, coastal motorboats and several types of harbour launches. So there was at least an experienced core of specialists for constructing the type of ships required by the navy.

This page: Although life had to continue despite four air raids during a single night, there were some aspects which came to a crashing halt. Just imagine coming to work one morning and finding scenes like these. What would you do and how could you continue? Sadly some aspects such as the food supply chains for classified places like prison camps broke down completely either because the people providing the food were killed or their offices were destroyed. This then led to depravation on a huge scale and the victims, who had been bombed, were blamed after the War for not providing the necessary provisions.

The basic technical statistics for these fire-fighting ships were as follows:

Size:	60-70 tons
Power:	150-200-hp diesel engine for turning the propeller and for working centrifugal pumps
Speed:	12 knots
Pumps:	2
Pump power:	A maximum of about 18,000 litres per minute. Water could be sucked out of the sea through some large filtered entry channels or a special suction pipe could also be attached. The entire system was versatile enough to supply land-based fire fighters with water through a pipe several hundred metres long
Crew:	One warrant officer as commander and one warrant officer or chief petty officer as engineer plus a crew of about twelve with two men qualified as divers

Each boat carried enough equipment to remain away from base for several days at a time and was self-sufficient during this period. The vessels turned out to be jolly effective.

CHAPTER 12
Sentries and Guards

The lonely sentry guarding the coast! Photos like this appeared in abundance on all sides throughout the War to reinforce the comforting thought that the population was securely protected and well looked after. The propaganda systems supplemented such reassuring pictures with stories of brave men, up to their knees in muck and bullets, being given the biggest of medals. This created a large spearhead of celebrity soldiers, who occupied similar positions to television personalities of today. Everybody knew their name and took every opportunity to worship their achievements. Yet life for the ordinary soldier was different. In reality there were many more men standing idle or doing ordinary mundane jobs; without them the heroes of the front line would never have achieved their glamorous results. The armed forces knew full well that 'the devil makes work for idle hands' and therefore ensured that the thousands of men standing idle were kept busy, even if they were engaged in pointless jobs or just keeping up appearances. Standing guard on some forlorn beach waiting for an invasion was a good way of occupying those men who had nothing to do other than to wait for nothing to happen.

Not all of the daily routine was designed to keep idle hands occupied; a show of strength was also necessary to maintain a grip in occupied countries and there was nothing more impressive than a military parade. There was relatively little crime and for much of the time there was hardly any sabotage against occupying forces, so such shows of strength were probably quite effective. They usually attracted a crowd of onlookers, even in the more hostile occupied areas.

The above picture is most interesting as part of a signpost has been included. In case the words are not clear, they say: Breda 37, ...tterdam (Rotterdam) 85 in one direction and ...len 7, ...stad 29 in the other direction. Bearing in mind that motorways were not built until long after the War and that such parades often took place in the town centre, it is possible to work out the exact location of this parade. Google Maps will even provide some modern views of this spot with the buildings in this picture still standing.

Opposite below: Despite many modern adverts with flashing lights and thumping noises, no one has ever invented anything more effective than flying flags for impressing people and announcing the fact that 'we are here'. Adding a few imposing guards, even if they are there only for decoration rather than protection, goes a long way to strengthen the message. Even today, such military displays of strength still make major tourist attractions and they also played a vital role during the Second World War.

Above: Not all guards had such glamorous jobs as standing in front of impressive headquarters and there were many boring checkpoints where guards did nothing more than glance at passes during their four-hour spell on duty. This photograph could have been taken anywhere in Europe, even England if it was not for the guards' distinctive helmets. The lorry hurtling along the dusty lane certainly gives no indication whether it is driving on the left or right. The chevrons on the side of the sentry's box are of interest because these have given rise to considerable debate at various recent re-enactment shows. All the pictures found in the German U-boat Museum show naval chevrons as seen in this photo, although it is possible that other non-naval units had them the other way up.

Next page, above: Another set of essential guards who were not there for decoration. This shows the approach to the U-boat piers in Kiel with their wooden trellises to provide some rudimentary camouflage against aircraft. The notice on the left states that people must have a special pass when visiting the (5th) flotilla area. 'Through Traffic is Prohibited'. The other notice to the right states that photography is prohibited and cameras must be deposited with the guards. Despite such stringent rules and photographing being a court martial offence, thousands of photographs were taken during the War, indicating that the men did not take too much notice of the rules.

The majority of ships and boats carried an array of sidearms and provided their own guards in port. These usually had nothing to do and carried a gun or wore a belt with a pistol or bayonet only to indicate that they were in fact the duty guard. Everyone reported to the guard when leaving the boat or coming aboard, but only legitimate people would have managed to get past the port's security screen, so such guards didn't have much to do and wandered around, hoping time would pass more quickly. They were not allowed to smoke, sit or lean against anything. Guards found to be sitting were automatically given a few days in solitary confinement, but naval punishment cells were more comfortable than the interior of U-boats and E-boats.

Left: With everything in short supply during the War, pilfering became an acceptable pastime for many and effective guards, rather than stationary sentries, became a vital part of many naval operations, both on land and at sea. This shows part of the luggage sheds of the naval base in Kiel with a guard at the gate. The personal belongings of men at sea were packed in cases and stored in sheds like these. They were numbered with the men's field post number and lorry loads of bags would be moved from one base to another to be ready for when the men arrived there. This provided ideal opportunities for thieves and guarding such places was most important.

CHAPTER 13
Air Raid Shelters

The thought of building air raid shelters was considered to have been subversive until after the start of the War when it became clear that the Luftwaffe did not have the power to defend vulnerable targets from Allied bombers. Before the Second World War the navy did place a few vital communication centres, ammunition stores and fuel tanks under concrete and often disguised these with a thin veneer of bricks to make them look like ordinary buildings, but the majority of bunkers were not started until after the beginning of the War.

The requirements for such bunkers varied considerably and very little has been written about them, but in recent years a number of energetic groups have emerged throughout Germany to study the history of these lifesaving buildings and to maintain some as serious monuments. (Flak Towers and the biggest bunkers, such as those capable of holding submarines or motor torpedo boats, have been omitted because they would need a book on their own to do them justice.)

People at home and civilians in general had to make best use of whatever bunkers were available for them, but there didn't seem to be a shortage of spaces. Yet despite this, some bunkers in already heavily bombed areas were over-crowded and people hurried past emptier bunkers nearer home because they argued that bombers were less likely to attack areas that had already been destroyed. The types of bunkers varied considerably. Wilhelmshaven with its water table only a few metres below ground level was dominated by high bunkers, while tube bunkers were provided in dryer towns. These were made from huge concrete pipes buried deep underground, usually two or three side by side and with substantial concrete entrances at each end. These were often under parks or gardens close to offices or blocks of flats. Many of these are still in situ today. The entrances were demolished after the war and covered with soil. At least one of the huge underground bunkers on the Reeperbahn in Hamburg now serves as underground parking garage. The majority of houses in Germany were originally built with cellars and many of these had their ceilings reinforced with old railway rails to support the weight of a collapsed building while the basement served as makeshift air raid shelter.

The big problem with general air raid shelters was that they stood empty until the alarm sounded and then they had to be filled as quickly as possible, often by thousands of people. This introduced a great conflict of interests into the design. On the one hand

The fact that German bunkers were of a high quality can be illustrated with this picture of the naval base in Lorient, where everything has been demolished except for the bunker in the middle. It was not until the end of the War, when Barnes Wallis designed new concrete breaking bombs, that these bastions were seriously challenged. However, the specifications for some of the early air raid shelters were too weak and a good number succumbed to Allied bombs, often killing masses of people inside them. Those bunkers that survived the War stood up well to bombing and after the war the Allied armies of occupation had great problems when they tried demolishing this stark evidence of their crass and incredibly inhuman bombing campaign.

The Flandern Bunker by one of the main gates to the naval dockyard in Kiel is a typical example of what command bunkers looked like. It was given this name because the field on which it stood had that title since the Kaiser's times. The naval base was considerably bigger during the Second World War and then the bunker was well within the military boundaries. There must have been some rather special machinery inside, probably advanced radios with their own generators, otherwise the Army of Occupation would not have cut those massive holes into the walls to remove the contents. These huge holes in the thick walls have now been blocked with large glass panels to turn what was a ruin into an attractive museum.

Right: For some reason one of the air locks of the Flandern Bunker was cut open after the War, probably to remove some long object, which could not be rotated to fit through the comparatively narrow entrance with such tight corners. This wide-angle panorama also shows that another similar hole was cut into the top floor and note that the air lock by the side of the main bunker had two doors leading into the interior.

Below: Although bunkers were often fitted with emergency lighting, there were times when the interior was thrown into total darkness for long periods. Walls were painted white to help make the dingy interior less forbidding. This shows one of the two command bunkers at the Bant U-boat Base in Wilhelmshaven.

The important point about command bunkers was that the small staffs of essential support units were often incarcerated inside them for long periods. Yet dockyards also employed masses of people in widespread offices who also needed protection during air raids. With half a dozen or more such warnings each day, it would have been too detrimental if all the staff stopped work to hurry to the nearest shelter. To alleviate such time wasting problems many essential offices had bunkered sections added to them. This meant there was no need for the staff to react to the first, say about 20 minute, warning of approaching aircraft. Observers, usually on the roof, would sound a full alert on their own internal alarm if it looked as they were going to become a target. At that point people could take their work with them and squeeze into the bunkered section attached to the corners of the office block. At the same time important papers could be kept in safe places.

the smallest possible armoured doors provided better protection than huge openings and on the other such small entrances provided real bottlenecks.

Inadvertently, some bunkers became dreadful death traps. For example one large bunker in Hamburg had only one door opening outwards so that any blast should force it tighter shut rather than blow it open. On one occasion a bomb blew a large cement mixer across the street to jam it against the door, making it impossible to open from the inside. Incendiaries then created massive fires around the bunker, to literally slowly cook the people inside. It was several days before it became cool enough for the first civil defence workers to reach it and all they could do was to seal the door for several months until enough men with gas masks and transport could be assembled to clear the pungent mess.

The problem of getting in and out of bunkers was solved by having a number of separate units within one bunker so that people entering through one door could not interfere with others coming through a different entrance. The inside was then so arranged that people walked as far as they could before settling on a seat. Of course, many people knew that their homes might be destroyed during the air raid and therefore came as if going on holiday with a lot of luggage, carrying many essential items of clothing, food, blankets and some knitting to pass long hours. Reading was difficult because the interiors were often dingy. Some light bulbs were usually missing and special bunker bulbs were produced with unique markings so that they could be identified when stolen. These were, of course, most vulnerable and there was a general shortage. Together with windows, light bulbs were among the first air raid casualties; even blasts quite a long way off would break glass.

This sixteen-pointed air raid shelter in Wilhelmshaven is now being preserved as a national monument and can be visited by appointment. This type was also built as circular structures, often with a layer of bricks on the outside and sometimes even with a covering of roofing tiles. The rounded shape stood up better to heavy blasts than flat walls. The details of this shelter are as follows:

Location: Norderneystrasse on corner with Minsener Oog

Built:	1940
Diameter:	16.2 metres
Thickness of walls:	1.4 metres
Thickness of roof:	3 metres
Inside:	8 floors with 4 staircases

Made from Ferro-concrete

Capacity:	1,500 adults

A bunker at Sande, close to Wilhelmshaven, where the post-war demolition process failed most miserably. It is now being used by a mountaineering club and has an artificial climbing wall built onto it, while the inside serves as club house.

The roof of the massive Valentin Bunker at Farge bear Bremen, built to accommodate an assembly line for the new electro-submarines of Type XXI, showing a hole blown by one of Barnes Wallis's special bunker breaking bombs. This massive tangle of iron and concrete illustrates the intricate composition of Ferro-concrete.

Many people chose not to make use of air raid shelters and took up positions on roofs to deal with the many incendiary bombs being dropped in residential areas. This was quickly frustrated by both the British and American air forces scattering vast quantities of phosphorous over residential areas or spraying large areas with a highly flammable oily liquid. These maimed and slowly killed thousands of civilians as they made their way to air raid shelters. Later the bombing became so intensive that extra precautions had to be taken to protect those essential characters, such as fire reporters and guards, who were expected to remain at their posts despite the ever-increasing infernos. As a result a number of small special bunkers were made, often on a local scale, and placed in vulnerable areas. In some areas these small one to six-man bunkers were removed, but a good number in the Hamburg Freeport remained where they had stood until the early 1980s. Sadly most of these brilliant little lifesavers have now vanished and hardly any remain in museums.

Above: This small five-man bunker originally stood in the naval dockyard of Wilhelmshaven. It was dropped into the water after the War when those buildings not damaged by wartime bombing were demolished by the army of occupation. Now it is probably the only survivor of its type and can be seen at the bunker museum in Norderneystrasse. At the moment this museum is only open by appointment, but this and several one-man shelters can be viewed through the fence from the road.

Right: A one-man shelter on display in Wilhelmshaven.

At one time there were a large number of one-man bunkers by the side of the Elbe II submarine bunker in Hamburg's Vulkanhafen, but this site has now been redeveloped as a massive container terminal and both the bunkers and much of the old anti-submarine netting, converted to serve as fencing, has now disappeared. The doors to these small structures were most substantial and trying to open them in the early 1980s proved most difficult without a good dose of oil to ease the thick rust.

CHAPTER 14
Rules for Living in Naval Barracks

All aspects of life in the armed forces, right down to the exact position where items had to be placed inside a locker, were governed by rules and regulations. To make sure these were understood, the navy produced a vast number of rulebooks. Some of them were typed on A4 pages, but the majority were properly printed as pocket-sized editions and produced by leading publishers. Although the general text in them is roughly identical, there appears to be no logical order in which the regulations were presented and some aspects were repeated several times on different pages using different words, almost as if the authors became paranoid about certain subjects. The rules are difficult to follow, incredibly boring to read and the following is nothing more than a brief summary. As far as possible the original word sequences have been kept to preserve the style, although this makes some passages even more difficult to understand. One wonders how new recruits managed it, but in those days the majority of people left school with the ability to read, write and to cope with elementary arithmetic.

All unmarried men not accommodated aboard a ship, lived in naval barracks either on land or in accommodation ships. Married men, not in married quarters, were allowed to live outside the naval complex, although it was often the case that one flat had to be shared by two or more families. The navy usually rented ordinary civilian flats or houses privately and the men themselves did not have to find their own quarters. However, many, especially men from the higher ranks, preferred to live away from naval controls and did find their own homes.

Many buildings within the naval bases had originally been built under the Kaiser during the late 1800s and they were bursting at the seams by the time the Second World War started. Pressures created by the war expansion meant that even more space was needed and this situation was eased when it became apparent that temporarily laid-up passenger ships were going to remain idle for much longer than anticipated and could therefore be modified and pressed into service. Air travel at that time was still very much in its infancy and reserved for the super rich. The majority of people would have travelled in large ships with accommodation for almost every pocket, from luxurious first class to rough and ready steerage for those with little money. Lying idle due to the hostilities, these ships were ideal for solving the navy's accommodation problems. This worked reasonably well

Naval accommodation varied dramatically in the occupied countries and in places it was quite luxurious. 'Adding some curtains and hanging some pictures on the wall,' said the regulations, 'will go a long way to making the barracks more homely.'

and many of them provided excellent facilities. Hurriedly erected wooden huts, often well insulated and reasonably comfortable were also used once the War started.

Passenger ships were built for speed and although their claim of being unsinkable had gone down with the *Titanic* in 1912, the shipping lines did pride themselves on making their ships as safe as possible by dividing the hull into a number of watertight compartments. Once below, passengers could not walk from one end of the ship to the other. The only exit from those confined spaces was up comparatively narrow and steep companionways and these provided an ideal trapping system if the upper decks started burning during an air attack. Strangely enough, these huge monsters located in easily detectable positions were not often hit, but there were a few horrific cases where men were killed because they were literally roasted alive. What is more, some of the fires were started not by the enemy but by something as innocuous as a film projector overheating.

Although many of these liners were equipped with exceedingly high levels of sophistication and luxury, once the War started Germany could no longer supply enough fuel to run the machinery for powering the heating systems. As a result, there were many cases of men finding the towels in the washrooms frozen stiff during cold winter mornings. It might also be interesting to add that many liners from the pre-war period had foreign names and ships like *Milwaukee*, *Monte Sarmiento* and *Monte Rosa* did, in fact, belong to German shipping lines.

Whether land or ship-based the navy wanted the barracks to become the sailors' second home, where they could live comfortably and be happy. Consequently men were free to decorate the rooms to suit their taste, so that they would be proud of their home. 'A good lampshade, attractive curtains and some interesting pictures on the wall will help,' said the regulations. 'And then happiness and cheerfulness will do the rest.'

Although this may sound most liberal, the regulations also stated that living together with so many people in comparatively confined spaces demanded a great deal of consideration and meticulous subordination. The pressures created by such demands had to be accepted by all men as being a necessary part of the comradeship between individuals. It was vitally important that sailors did not obey the regulations out of fear of being punished, but because they realized that orderly behaviour makes it easier to live together in close-knit

The sailors' mess at the U-boat School in Neustadt (Schleswig Holstein) gives a good picture of the overcrowding in some of the barracks. There wasn't much room for anyone who wasn't prepared to fit in. Yet, despite the lack of space many men said that the food was usually pretty good.

One of the reading or common rooms at the naval barracks. Usually there were plenty of books, magazines and newspapers, although their subject matter was sometimes limited to what the officer in charge thought best to supply.

communities. The men had to be fully aware of the fact that cleanliness, order and respect for other people's property were vital. Older soldiers were expected to set an example to younger men, provide them with the support they needed and demonstrate how to behave, how to react and how to deport themselves around the naval base.

Each base had special dining rooms for men to eat their midday meals; it was pointed out in the regulations that every person must attend in decent clothes and with clean hands. Barracks also had canteens where men could have bought, for cash, daily necessities at especially low prices. It had to be clearly understood that alcoholic drinks could only be consumed in the canteen's rooms and were not allowed be taken out. It was against the rules to store or consume drinks in bedrooms.

Every man who was not inside the barracks by lights-out had to have an appropriate leave pass and after the sounding of the last post he had to enter the military complex only through the main gate. Anyone who attempted to get into the barracks by side entrances was likely to be punished. Total silence was expected at lights-out and any men returning late had to come in silently without disturbing their colleagues. It might be interesting to add that some naval bases were surrounded by high walls, but many were open for anyone to wander in and out at will. The strange point was that the side gates were often left open all night and any unsavoury character could have walked in. Yet, despite such openness there were hardly any infringements.

Collecting money for parties or for any other reason was allowed only with permission of the company commander and all forms of gambling, including playing games of chance, were prohibited. At the same time men were not allowed to sell or distribute anything, whether it be goods or reading matter. Men were not allowed to keep large sums of money, but the regulations did not specify the limits. Larger sums of money had to be handed to the duty officer for safekeeping.

The rules emphasized that it was of utmost importance for everybody to project a decent impression towards the outside and therefore soldiers were not allowed to dry clothing or gloves in windows. Men were not allowed to lean out of windows nor look out of them to watch something happening outside. Shouting and any form of excessive noise that might offend passers-by had to be avoided. However, that did not include singing and making music during free time, but the use of signalling equipment and slamming doors did definitely not fit into the daily routine.

Beds had to be made immediately after getting up, mattresses turned over and the straw sacks shaken. Although the navy made use of blankets at sea, on land they tended to provide empty duvet covers for filling with hay or more often straw. This was nothing unusual for the armed forces and many of the poorer families within the country would have slept under similar conditions. Beds had to be made so that all of them looked identical and generally men were not allowed to lie on them during the day. People on night shifts and men with minor injuries or illnesses were excluded, but they had to remove their shoes or boots before lying on their bed. Smoking in bed was strictly prohibited.

Heating stoves in each room had to be burned out by lights-out because otherwise there was a danger of fire or men being overcome by noxious gasses. (There were very few buildings with central heating in those days.) Using electricity for any other purpose than those directed by the navy was prohibited and anyone found plugging unofficial items into the system was treated the same as a thief.

Cartridges, gunpowder, explosives and all other flammable substances were not allowed in living quarters and had to be deposited with the warrant officer responsible for shooting. Later during the War and especially in foreign countries, when it became common for officers and non-commissioned officers to carry sidearms, they were often allowed to keep the ammunition issued for their weapon.

The Book of Rules emphasized that one of the best ways of judging the quality of a soldier is to look inside his locker. The outside had to be labelled with the soldier's name and the inside arranged according to the regulations. When away from the room and at night the lockers had to be locked; leaving property lying around in the room was not allowed. Dirty washing had to be washed or handed in for cleaning at the earliest possible time. It was against the rules to keep exceedingly filthy clothing inside the locker and each locker had to be emptied and scrubbed at least once a week. Special attention had to be paid to the storing of food inside lockers.

The most senior man in each room was responsible for keeping everything in good order and checking regularly that everybody in his charge was abiding by the regulations. He also had to appoint one person (or two if it was an exceptionally large room) to be

The higher naval ranks fared a bit better for space than the ordinary sailors and some warrant and commissioned officers had most appealing accommodation.

One of the rooms in the accommodation area of the Flag Officer for U-boats in Angers, in the west of France.

Wooden huts constructed out of fire resisting chemicals became a common feature during the War and many of them were hidden in gardens to prevent them from becoming obvious targets for bombers.

More permanent brick or stone buildings were also provided in some naval bases.

Blackout curtains were a feature of everyday life and the fact that this room has a filing cabinet, a safe and a telephone suggests it is an official office, rather than someone's private quarters.

Keeping fit and playing games was strongly supported by the authorities; preparing for serious matches was just as important to many men as dealing with their daily work.

on duty each day and that person had to be easily identifiable from the list on the door. This person was not allowed to leave the barracks during his spell on duty and was responsible for keeping everything clean and in working order. His day usually started by fetching early morning coffee, waking the rest of the men and in winter cleaning the stove in order to relight it for the day. Once everybody was up and dressed, he was responsible for opening the windows and airing the room as well as checking for dust under the beds and in corners. Even at the beginning of the Second World War there were still barracks built before the introduction of piped water and therefore also without drains. So, the soldier on duty had to take any dirty washing water to the wet pits in the yard.

Although there was plenty of emphasis on cleaning, scrubbing and washing, the men were warned that they must use as little water as possible and under no circumstances were they allowed to spray water around as if they were onboard ship. Pouring buckets of water over floors was also prohibited to prevent the joists from rotting. It was not permitted to wash clothing in living rooms and anything wet had to be taken up to a specially designated drying loft. Washrooms were provided for the sole purpose of washing bodies and no one was allowed to clean clothing or scrub equipment in there.

These rules – hundreds of pages of them – encompassed every aspect of life and included every conceivable subject. They may sound rough, demeaning and at times incredibly clumsy, but they were designed to make a difficult life bearable and there are many examples where they go out of their way to help the men. For example, married men were allowed to have sexual intercourse with their wife but non-married men seeking sexual intercourse had to wear a condom when doing so and these were supplied free of charge by the authorities. What is more, the navy kept a record of everybody who requested a condom, but used only the soldier's identification number instead of his name. So it was almost impossible for casual observers to find who was on his way to the brothel.

CHAPTER 15
German Naval Bases

(In the approximate order as the names appear on maps)

- The majority of the German names used 'Marine' (Navy or Naval) as a prefix. This has been omitted from the following table to prevent massive repetition and thus make it easier to read.
- The general term 'department' in the following table could also be translated as 'unit', 'division', 'section' or 'detachment'.
- 'Radio Station' refers to bigger stations with facilities for intercepting and decoding enemy radio traffic, manned mainly by naval personnel from the B-Dienst or Radio Monitoring Service.
- Flotillas with operational units of the Fleet Command or other operational front flotillas have not been included, nor have flotillas under the jurisdiction of the Security Forces (Sicherheitsverbände).
- The units listed below may not have been present for the whole of the War and temporary positions of a few months in duration have been omitted.
- Most of the guns along the German coast have not been included. In all there were about 200 heavy guns, but only very little evidence of their existence remains.

Opposite: Tirpitz lying inside her ring of torpedo and submarine nets. The Norwegian fjords made admirable parking places for a number of large naval units and for merchant ships running the blockade. Many of these fjords were so isolated and so well hidden that there was no land-based naval backup nearby.

The mine depot in Tromso (Norway) with a man carrying a basket of eggs. Such heavy objects were usually delivered by supply ship and deposited wherever there was room until minelayers were available to take them on board.

A wrecked ship lying alongside one of the iron ore-loading quays in Narvik (Norway). Scenes like this presented the transport system with a logistical nightmare because some harbours were so jammed up with sunken wrecks that careful planning was necessary to accommodate any ships coming in with vital supplies.

GERMANY	
Borkum	Radio Station Port Protection Flotilla Artillery Detachment 116 Air Spotter Department 216 Island Battalion 350
Juist	Island Battalion 355
Norderney	Artillery Detachment 126 Air Spotter Department 226
Wangerooge	Artillery Detachment 112, 132 & 631 Air Spotter Department 232 2. Light Flak Training Division
Helgoland	Island Commander Artillery Detachment 122 Air Spotter Department 242
Leer	8. Ship Crew Training Department 18. Reserve Department 2. Reserve Women Auxiliaries Corps Artillery Detachment 126
Emden	VI. Artillery Division 6. Reserve Artillery Division Fortress Engineer Battalion 360 8. Vehicle Division 6. Air Spotter Regiment Air Spotter Department 236
Westerhusen	Air Spotter Department 266
Aurich	42. Reserve Division
Norden	8. Reserve Department 2. Driver Training Department 10. Artillery Division
Wittmund	30. Ship Crew Training Department
Jever	Naval Offices
Wilhelmshaven	Major Naval Base
Varel	6. Training Department 4. Reserve Department
Nordenham	Fortress Battalion 362
Brake	12. Ship Crew Training Department

Bremen	34. Reserve Department
Farge	36. Reserve Department
Bremerhaven	2. Ship Crew Training Regiment 10. Ship Crew Training Department 2. Training Regiment 4. Training Department Non-Commissioned Officer Training Department Air Spotter Department 244 & 264 Alarm Battalion 21
Nordholz	Radio Station
Cuxhaven	4. Reserve Regiment 12. Reserve Department IV. Artillery Division Artillery Detachment 114 8. Reserve Artillery Division (Altenwalde) 4. Reserve Artillery Division Air Spotter Department 214 Port Protection Flotilla 4. Vehicle Division Construction Battalion 314 Fortress Battalion 359 (Altenbruch) Training Battalion (Alarm Battalion)
Balje	Air Spotter Department 294
Stade	Naval Offices
Buxtehude	18. Ship Crew Training Department
Hamburg	31. U-Flotilla 32. U-Flotilla 32. Reserve Department
Glückstadt	14. Ship Crew Training Department
Brunsbüttel	2. Canal Watch Department 14. Air Spotter Regiment
Sandhayn	Air Spotter Department 254
Büsum	Naval Offices
Tönning	Fortress Battalion 357
Friedrichstadt	Artillery Detachment 124
Schwesing	7. Reserve Department

Husum	Fortress Engineer Staff Vehicle Department 8. Reserve Artillery Division
Lütjenholm	7. Training Department
Pellworm	Island Commander
Föhr	22. Reserve Department Island Commander
Amrum	Fog Making Department 353 Island Commander
Sylt Hörnum	6. Reserve Department
Sylt Westerland	5. Reserve Department Air Spotter Department 234 Island Battalion 351 Artillery Detachment 134 8. Air Spotter Regiment Air Spotter Department 204 & 234
Sylt List	Training Command 700 Midget Weapons Unit Radio Station
Flensburg	1. Training Division for New Warship Construction 1. Female Naval Auxiliaries Reserve Division School for Female Auxiliary Leaders
Mürwik	Officers School Torpedo School
Glücksburg	1. Training Regiment
Geltringer Bucht	U-boats scuttled at end of War
Kappeln	Training Division for Midget Weapons Unit
Falshöft	Radio Station
Schleswig	3. U-boat Acceptance Command
Eckernförde	Torpedo Trials Institute 5. Ship Crew Training Department 1. Training Regiment Air Spotter Department 211
Kiel	Major Base
Laboe	Naval Memorial
Möltenort	U-boat Memorial

Narvik Harbour with an abundance of shipping. Getting ships into action hot spots was sometimes exceedingly difficult and at times there were no alternatives to using dolphin berths and unloading cargoes into barges. It was not only military supplies that were held up, but also daily supplies being imported for the local population.

One problem was that military action could take place some distance from main population centres and the small centres could not accommodate the masses brought in to fight the War. As a result many inadequate quarters had to be used. This shows the old Viking in Narvik being used as accommodation for U-boat crews. Apparently it was quite comfortable inside and provided considerably better conditions than the men were used to in their U-boats.

Rendsburg	3. Canal Watch Department 5. Training Division for New Warship Construction Air Spotter Department 231 & 243
Neumünster	Offices for Eastern Command Radio Station
Plön	1. U-boat Acceptance Command Midget Weapons Units
Malente	Medical Examination Centre for U-boat Crews
Eutin	Offices
Neustadt	1. U-boat Training Division 3. U-boat Training Division 2. U-boat Acceptance Command Midget Weapons Unit Training Department
Travemünde	Naval Offices
Lübeck	Fortress Battalion 357
Schlutup	Training Command for Midget Weapons Unit
Warnemünde	26. U-Flotilla before end of war
Rostock	Naval Offices
Stralsund	7., 9. & 11. Ship Crew Training Department 3. Training Regiment 32. Ship Crew Training Department
Dänholm	Selection and Initial Training for Officer Candidates
Rügen	Fortress Engineer Staff 7 (also Bornholm) Air Spotter Department 227 Cape Arkona Radio Station
Suhrendorf	Midget Weapons Unit (Training)
Sassnitz	Island Commander Rügen Air Spotter Department 213
Bornholm	Light Artillery Detachment 535 U-boat Sound Detection Unit Fortress Engineer Staff 7
Waren	9. Reserve Department Naval Troops Camp Weapons Unit
Neustrelitz	3. Reserve Regiment 19. & 25. & 3. Reserve Department

Stavanger Harbour with a group of modern German minesweepers.

This appears to be Larvik in southern Norway with a variety of ships in the harbour.

Ahlbeck	Radar Department Pomerania (Pommern)
Swinemünde (Swinoujscie)	15. Reserve Department Fortress Construction Staff Coast Protection Flotilla Harbour Commander III. Artillery Division
	3. Reserve Artillery Division Artillery Detachment 123 Commander Sea Defences Pomerania (Pommern) Fortress Engineer Staff 8 Reconnaissance Staff 3. Air Spotters Regiment Air Spotter Department 233, 711 & 713 3. Vehicle Division
Stettin (Szczecin)	4. U-Flotilla 33. Reserve Department
Wollin (Wolinski)	Light Artillery Detachment 536
Kolberg (Kolobrzeg)	Liaison Officer East Pomerania (Pommern) Air Spotter Department 243
Flatow (Zlotow)	17. Reserve Department
Deutsch Krone (Walcz)	23. Ship Crew Training Department 3. Reserve Artillery Detachment
Stolpmünde (Ustka)	Radio Station
Leba (Leba)	21. Ship Crew Training Department
Hela (Hel)	Training Unit for U-boats going to the Front 15. Reserve Artillery Division Artillery Detachment 119 Air Spotter Department 818
Gotenhafen (Gdynia)	2nd U-boat Training Division 24. U-Flotilla before end of war 27. U-Flotilla Tactical Training Harbour Master 9. Reserve Artillery Division 13. Reserve Artillery Division Artillery Detachment 629 9. Air Spotter Regiment Air Spotter Department 219, 229, 249 & 259 1. Fog Making Department 5. Air Spotters Division 35. Reserve Department

Zopport (Soport)	Naval Offices
Danzig (Gdansk)	Air Spotter Department 229 8. U-Flotilla 23. U-Flotilla (Commander shooting training) 24. U-Flotilla (Commander shooting training and later underwater detection training) 25. U-Flotilla (Shooting training) Special Command 7000
Deutsch Eylau (Ilawa)	11. Reserve Artillery Division
Elbing (Elblag)	U-boat building and repairs
Pillau (Baltijsk)	3. U-boat Acceptance Command 19. U-Flotilla (Commanders' initial training and Lookout School) School for Basic boat handling for docking 20. U-Flotilla (Tactical training) 26. U-Flotilla (Shooting training) 5. Ships Crews Training Regiment 25. Ship Crew Training Department Coastal Commander Eastern Baltic Fortress Engineer Staff Harbour Master V. Artillery Division 5. Reserve Artillery Division Artillery Detachment 115 & 533 Air Spotter Department 215 & 225 Special Command 7000 Radio Station
Königsberg (Kalingrad)	8. U-Flotilla 32. U-Flotilla 37. Reserve Department
Memel (Klaipeda)	4. U-boat Training Division 24. U-Flotilla later in War 21. Reserve Department Port Protection Flotilla VII. Artillery Division Artillery Detachment 117 Air Spotter Department 217 17. Ship Crew Training Department

Libau (Liepaja)	3. Ship Crew Training Regiment 9. Vehicle Division Commander C 1. Intelligence Department Commander for Sea Defences Harbour Master 7. Reserve Artillery Detachment Air Spotter Department 239, 712 Naval Dockyard Coast protection Flotilla Ostland Sea Commander Lettland (Latvia)
Windau (Ventspils)	Harbour Master 31. Ship Crew Training Department
Riga (Riga)	Sea Commander Harbour Master Supply Depot
Reval (Tallin)	Sea Transport Commander East 9. & 3. Vehicle Divisions 3. Driver Training Division Fortress Engineer Battalion 321 Harbour Master Artillery Detachment 530 & 532 Air Spotter Department 239 & 711 Supply Base Naval Arsenal

NORTH RUSSIA	
Teriberka	Harbour Commander until the end 1940 Located to the east of Murmansk
Litza Fjord	Located west of Murmansk

NORWAY	
Kirkeness	Naval Base Radio Station Commander of Sea Defences Harbour Master Port / Coast Protection Flotilla Sea Transport Centre 3 x 150-mm Guns

Lorries parked outside the naval command office in Larvik (Norway). Although there were bigger vehicles, these must rank among the largest road transport of the time.

Mestersand	4 x 240-mm Guns
Vadsø	3 x 130-mm Guns
Kieberg	3 x 280-mm Guns
Vardø	Harbour Master Artillery Detachment 513
Tana	3 x 130-mm Guns
Honningsvaag	Harbour Master Artillery Detachment 514
Nordkap	3 x 170-mm Guns
Porsanger	3 x 130-mm Guns
Fuglenes	4 x 110-mm Guns
Hammerfest	Naval Base Radio Station Commander of Sea Defences Harbour Master Port / Coast Protection Flotilla Artillery Detachment 514 Artillery Detachment 710 3 x 130-mm Guns
Alta	Harbour Master 3 x 130-mm Guns
Lyngen	4 x 150-mm Guns
Karlsøy	4 x 150-mm Guns
Tromsø	Major Naval Base Radio Station Commander of Sea Defences Harbour Master Naval Supply Depot Air Spotter Department 710 3 x 105-mm Guns
Tromsdalen	Artillery Detachment 512
Bergfjord	6 x 155-mm Guns
Skrolsvik	4 x 150-mm Guns

Germans inspecting the entrance of the torpedo tunnel at Oskarborg (Norway). The torpedoes used to sink the German heavy cruiser *Blücher* were launched from this antiquated defence system.

The business end of the torpedo tunnel at Oskarborg (Norway), guarding the approaches to the capital, Oslo.

Harstad	Naval Base Radio Station Harbour Master Artillery Regiment Headquarters Artillery Detachment 511 Air Spotter Department 709
Kilbotn	Air Spotter Department 823
Narvik	Major Naval Base Radio Station Commander of Sea Defences Harbour Master Port / Coast Protection Flotilla Air Spotter Department 706 & 710
Lødingen	Harbour Master Artillery Detachment 516 4 x 305-mm Guns, 1 x 150-mm Gun 4 x 88-mm AA Guns
Engeløy	Artillery Detachment 516 3 x 406-mm Guns, 3 x 210-mm Guns
Stamsund	Artillery Detachment 514
Reine	Artillery Detachment 514
Bodø	Harbour Master Radio Station
Mo	Radio Station 4 x 105-mm Guns
Mo I Rana	Harbour Master Naval Command Centre
Sandnessjøen	Naval Base Commander of Sea Defences Harbour Master Port / Coast Protection Flotilla Artillery Detachment 510 4 x 127-mm Guns
Mosjøen	Harbour Master Radio Station Naval Transport Centre from Nov. '44 4 x 120-mm Guns
Brønnøysund	Harbour Master
Rørvik	Harbour Master 4 x 127-mm Guns

Trondheim	Major Naval Base Radio Station Commander of Sea Defences Naval Command Centre Sea Transport Centre
	Construction Office Naval Arsenal 32. Air Spotter Regiment Air Spotter Department 701, 702 & 715
Brettingen	Artillery Detachment 506
Husøen	Artillery Detachment 507 3 x 280-mm Guns 4 x 88-mm AA Guns
Kristiansund	Harbour Master 3 x 150-mm Guns 4 x 88-mm AA Guns
Molde	Harbour Master Commander of Sea Defences Artillery Detachment 505
Andalsnes	Harbour Master
Alesund	Harbour Master Radio Station 3 x 150-mm Guns 4 x 88-mm AA Guns
Askevold	Harbour Master
Bergen	Major Naval Base Radio Station Commander of Sea Defences Harbour Master Naval Command Centre Sea Transport Centre Construction Office Naval Arsenal Air Spotter Regiment 822 from Nov. '44 6 x 210-mm Guns 3 x 240-mm Guns 1 x 105-mm Gun 4 x 150-mm Guns
Maaløy	Naval Offices
Haugesund	Harbour Master

Kopervik	Harbour Master Artillery Detachment 504
Leirvik Stord	Harbour Master
Stavanger	Major Naval Base Radio Station Commander of Sea Defences Naval Command Centre Harbour Master Naval Transport Centre Supply Depot Artillery Detachment Stavanger & 303 & 503
Egersund	Harbour Master
Randaberg	Naval guns
Kuiting Søy	4 x 170-mm Guns
Egersund	4 x 127-mm Guns
Farsund	Harbour Master
Kristiansand-Süd	Major Naval Base Radio Station Commander of Sea Defences Harbour Master Port / Coast Protection Flotilla Naval Transport Centre from Sep. '44 Naval Supply Depot Air Spotter Department 714 Artillery Detachment 502
Odderøya	Artillery Detachment 502 from 1942 4 x 240-mm Guns
Arendal	Harbour Master
Larvik	Harbour Master
Brevik	Harbour Master
Torød	Artillery Detachment 501
Horten	Major Naval Base Harbour Master Port / Coast Protection Flotilla Naval Arsenal Artillery Detachment 501

Haus Lemp near La Rochelle (France) was requisitioned as officer accommodation.

Dinner in Haus Lemp near La Rochelle (France) with Grand Admiral Karl Dönitz as guest.

Oslo	Supreme Naval Command Norway Major Naval Base Harbour Master Radio Station Port / Coast Protection Flotilla Naval Arsenal 3. Naval Flak Unit

DENMARK	
Copenhagen	Major Base Harbour Master Port / Coast Protection Flotilla Artillery Detachment 508, 522 & 525
Helsingør	Harbour Master Port / Coast Protection Flotilla
Hornbaek	4 x 120-mm Guns
Spodsbjerg	4 x 120-mm Guns
Hundested	Harbour Master
Nykøbing	Harbour Master
Gniben	4 x 150-mm Guns
Ravsnaes	4 x 120-mm Guns
Kalundborg	Harbour Master
Bornholm	Island Commander
Gedser	Harbour Master
Nakskow	Harbour Master
Korsør	Harbour Master
Nyborg	Harbour Master Port / Coast Protection Flotilla
Svendborg	Harbour Master
Ollerup	27. Ship Crew Training Department
Sonderborg	7. Reserve-Artillery Detachment
Fredericia	Harbour Master Port / Coast Protection Flotilla
Trelde Naes	4 x 105-mm Guns
Fyns Hoved	4 x 150-mm Guns

This page: Accommodation for U-boat men in La Pallice (France). Life onboard U-boats, motor torpedo boats and the like was very uncomfortable and therefore, while in port, crews were allocated land-based accommodation wherever possible.

Hansted	Artillery Detachment 118 Air Spotter Department 814
Arhus	Harbour Master Port / Coast Protection Flotilla Artillery Detachment 524 from Jan. '45 Air Spotter Department 717
Fornaes	4 x 110-mm Guns
Grenaa	Harbour Master Artillery Detachment 523 from Oct. '44
Aalborg	Harbour Master Port / Coast Protection Flotilla disbanded Oct. '43
Hals	Artillery Detachment 521 from Oct. '44
Frederikshavn	Commander North Jutland Harbour Master Port / Coast Protection Flotilla Air Spotter Department 716 from Nov. '44 Artillery Regiment 40 Artillery Detachment 509
Skagen	Harbour Master Port / Coast Protection Flotilla
Tverstedt	4 x 105-mm Guns
Hirtshals	Harbour Master
Hjörring	Radio Station
Løkken	4 x 150-mm Guns, 4 x 120-mm Guns
Thisted	Naval Supply Depot
Agger	4 x 120-mm Guns
Thyboren	Harbour Master
Esbjerg	Commander Danish West Coast Commander Sea Defences Skagen Harbour Master Port / Coast Protection Flotilla Supply Base Air Spotter Department 204 12 x 105-mm AA Guns
Fanø	Artillery Detachment 518 4 x 105-mm AA Guns

HOLLAND and BELGIUM	
Dutch North Sea Islands	Every island had a good number of anti-aircraft guns and many of them were manned by naval personnel
Dordrecht	Commander for Motorised Units in Holland from Sep. '42
Eindhoven	Naval Hospital
Utrecht	Naval Commander for the Netherlands Net Protection Flotilla North Sea / Holland 10. Vehicle Department 4. Radar Division from 1944
Amersfoort	Naval Arsenal
Harderwijk	Artillery und Flak Company
Delfzijl	Harbour Master 4 x 120-mm AA Guns Artillery Detachment 256
Termunten	4 x 105-mm AA Guns
Groningham	Harbour Master Sea Transport Commander Netherlands 6. Reserve Artillery Detachment later Steenwijk 4. Ship Crews Training Regiment 24 Ship Crew Training Department
Ameland	4 x 105-mm AA Guns
Harlingen	Harbour Master Port Protection Flotilla Air Spotter Department 246 Vehicle Department 246
Terschelling	Air Spotter Department 246
Vlieland	8 x 105-mm AA Guns
Texel – Eierland	4 x 105-mm AA Guns
Den Helder	Harbour Master Port Protection Flotilla There were an abundance of guns in the Den Helder area and many of them were manned by naval personnel
Hors	4 x 120-mm Guns
Egmont	4 x 105-mm Guns
Bergen	4 x 120-mm Guns
Camperdium	4 x 105-mm Guns

Amsterdam	Harbour Master Naval Training Division
Heiloo	Naval Offices
Wijk aan Zee	Artillery Detachment 201 4 x 150-mm Guns
Ijmuiden	Harbour Master Port Protection Flotilla Artillery Detachment 203 Air Spotter Department 816 There were over 100 bunkers in this area, many with large guns and many manned by naval personnel
Bloemendaal	Naval Commander for the Netherlands (end of War)
Noordwijk	4 x 150-mm Guns
Scheveningen	Naval Commander for the Netherlands Commander of Sea Defences for Central Holland 10. Vehicle Division
Den Haag	Naval Commander Netherlands – Belgium Several Command Headquarters Artillery Regiment 21
Vorburg	Commander of Sea Defences for Central Holland
Wassenaar	Naval Arsenal
Hoek van Holland	Harbour Master Port Protection Flotilla Artillery Detachment 205 Air Spotter Department 813
Rotterdam	Harbour Master Naval Command Office Supply Depot Naval Hospital
Bergen op Zoom	Naval Hospital Ship Crew Training Regiment 16 Ship Crew Training Department
Domburg	Artillery Detachment 202
Walcheren	Artillery Detachment 202

La Pallice receiving a good hammering from the Allied air forces, but with a good number of the bombs dropping harmlessly into the sea. This is where the docking scenes for the film *Das Boot* were shot and the U-boat bunker is just visible towards the bottom left. The majority of bombs seem to have missed it.

The German naval base at Constanta on the Black Sea with torpedo boats and a U-boat in the foreground.

Vlissingen	Commander of Sea Defences South Holland Harbour Master Port Protection Flotilla Artillery Detachment 202 Air Spotter Department 703 & 810
Antwerpen	Harbour Master Naval Command Centre Supply Depot Sea Commander for the Western Area
Zeebrugge	Harbour Master
Cadzand	Artillery Detachment 203
Breskens	Harbour Master Oct./Nov. '44 only
Le Coq de Haen	Artillery Regiment 22
Blankenberge	Artillery Detachment 206 until July '40
Ostende	Naval Base Artillery Detachment 204 1. Radar Division from Nov. '44
Nieuport	Harbour Master
Brugge	Naval Radar Department Flanders

NORTH EAST FRANCE	
Dunkirk	Harbour Master
Gravelines	Harbour Master
Calais	Major Naval Base Artillery Regiment 24
Sangatte /Cap Gris Nez	Artillery Detachment 242
Wimereux	Artillery Detachment 240
Boulogne	Major Naval Base Artillery Regiment 24
Le Treport	Harbour Master
Dieppe	Harbour Master Naval Supply Depot
Rouen	Harbour Master 20. Vehicle Department
Fecamp	Harbour Master

Above left: Hotel Royal was used for naval accommodation at St Nazaire.

Above right: This house in La Baule near St Nazaire was used as rest home by many U-boat men.

Below: Cars were often supplied to sea-going officers while they were in port. The badge of the snorting bull on the back of this car indicates that it is part of the vehicle pool of the 7th U-boat Flotilla and the letters WM show that it is an official vehicle belonging to the navy (Wehrmacht Marine – Armed Forces Navy).

Le Havre	Naval Base Artillery Detachment 266
Trouville	Harbour Master
Caen	Harbour Master
Cherbourg	Naval Base Artillery Detachment 260 & 608 22. Vehicle Department

CHANNEL ISLANDS	
Alderney	Harbour Master Artillery Detachment 604 & 605
Guernsey	Harbour Master Artillery Detachment 604 46. Minesweeper Flotilla
Jersey	Harbour Master 24. Minesweeper Flotilla

WEST FRANCE	
Granville	Harbour Master
St. Malo	Naval Base Artillery Detachment 608
Brest	Major Naval Base Artillery Detachment 262 Air Spotter Department 803, 804, 805, 811 & 231
Lorient	Major Naval Base Artillery Detachment 264 & 280 Air Spotter Department 806, 704, 708, 807, 817 & 818
Ile de Groix	Island Commander Light Artillery Detachment 681
Belle Island	Light Artillery Detachment 682, 683 & 688 Air Spotter Department 708
Carnac	Medical Research Centre for U-boats
St Nazaire	Major Naval Base Artillery Detachment 280, 703 Air Spotter Department 703, 809, 705, 819 & 820
Angers	Flag Officer for U-boats : West (FdU West)

Nantes	Harbour Master Construction Office 1. Intelligence Unit Air Spotter Department 819
Ille de Yeu	Island Commander Light Artillery Detachment 685
Les Sables d'Olonne	Harbour Master
Vendee Ile de Re	Artillery Detachment 282 & 684 Light Artillery Detachment 686 Air Spotter Department 812
La Pallice	Major Naval Base
La Rochelle	Harbour Master Vehicle Department
Rochefort	Harbour Master Naval Supply Depot Admiral Commanding West France later to Royan
Ile d'Oleron	Island Commander Light Artillery Detachment 687
Royan	Admiral Commanding West France Harbour Master Artillery Detachment 284
Gironde South	Port Protection Flotilla 2. Sperrbrecherflottille (Mine Detonating Flotilla) Artillery Detachment 284 (Nord Shore) 16. Vehicle Department
Pavillac	Harbour Master
Bordeaux	Major Naval Base
Arcachon	Harbour Master
Biarritz	Artillery Detachment 286
Bayonne	Harbour Master Artillery Detachment 286
San Jean de Luz	Harbour Master Artillery Detachment 286

SOUTH FRANCE	
Port Vendres	Harbour Master Artillery Detachment 615

Perpignan	Fortress Battalion 360
Sète	Artillery Arsenal Artillery Detachment 610
Montpellier	Harbour Master Radio Station
Port de Bouc	Harbour Master Artillery Detachment 615
Marseille	Naval Base Artillery Detachment 611
La Ciotat	Harbour Master
Toulon	Major Naval Base Radio Station Artillery Detachment 682 Air Spotter Department 819
Hyères	Naval Offices
St Topez	Harbour Master
Cannes	Harbour Master
Nice	Harbour Master

SPAIN	
Madrid	Radio Station
Seville	Radio Station

ITALY – ADRIATIC COAST	
San Remo	Harbour Master
Genoa	Naval Supply Depot Radio Station Sea Transport Centre Harbour Master 10. Torpedo Boat Flotilla Artillery Detachment 619 German Anti-Aircraft Units
Portofino	Naval Offices
Sestri Levante	Harbour Master
La Spezia	Naval Base Naval Arsenal

Piling up ammunition boxes outside an official building after it has been bombed. They could well contain explosives, but many empty boxes found their way into offices and workshops for storing essential items such as papers or tools.

The main gate of the Headquarters of the Flag Officer for U-boats West (FdU West) in Angers (France).

Magra Estuary	Naval Offices
Carrara	Radio Station
Viareggio	Harbour Master
Livorno	Harbour Master
Florence	Naval Arsenal
Rome	Sea Transport Centre Italy Radio Station
Naples	Anti-Aircraft Units Sea Transport Centre
Palermo	Sea Transport Centre
Cavallino	Artillery Detachment 634
Ancona	Harbour Master
Ravenna	Harbour Master
Adria	Minesweeping, S-Boot and other flotillas
Abbazia	Naval Offices
Chioggia	Artillery Detachment 633
Padua	Radio Station
Venice	Harbour Master Naval Arsenal Port Protection Flotilla 3. Escort Flotilla Minesweeping flotillas
Lido / Venice	Commander of Sea Defences West Adriatic
Opicina	Commander of Sea Defences Sea Transport Commander Adriatic 6. Transport Flotilla
Monfalcone	Commander of Sea Defences Air Spotter Department 730
Trieste	Naval Arsenal Harbour Master Sea Transport Centre Artillery Detachment 626 Air Spotter Department 821
Pola / Pula	Naval Arsenal Harbour Master Artillery Detachment 621 Escort and Motor Minesweeper Flotillas

A variety of naval offices.

Zadar	Harbour Master Artillery Detachment 540
Sibenik	Harbour Master
Split	Commander of Sea Defences Dalmatian Coast Harbour Master Artillery Detachment 628
Herceg-Novi	Naval Offices
Dubrovnik / Ragusa	Harbour Master Artillery Detachment 612
Durazzo / Tirana	Commander of Sea Defences Albania Harbour Master
Valona	Harbour Master

GREECE	
Korfu	Harbour Master
Kalami	Naval Offices
Argostoli / Kefallinia	Harbour Master
Patras	Commander of Sea Defences Western Greece Naval Base Artillery Detachment 617 Artillery Arsenal Sea Transport Centre
Pilos / Navarino	Harbour Master
Kalamata	Commander of Sea Defences Coastal Protection Flotilla
Monemvassia	Harbour Master
Nafplion / Nauplion	Harbour Master
Piräus	Harbour Master
Salamis	Naval Supply Depot and Repair Base Harbour Master Air Spotter Department 720
Athens	Naval Headquarters Radio Station
Egina	Artillery Detachment 603
Fleves	Artillery Detachment 621
Chalcis	Harbour Master

Volos	Harbour Master
Salonika	Commander of Sea Defences Northern Greece Harbour Master Coast Protection Flotilla Sea Transport Commander Vehicle Department
Mudros / Limnos	Commander of Sea Defences Limnos Harbour Master
Mytilene / Lebos	Harbour Master
Chios	Harbour Master
Samos	Harbour Master
Leros	Commander of Sea Defences Naval Base Harbour Master Artillery Detachment 624 Air Spotter Department Leros
Rhodos	Harbour Master
Dodekanes / Dodecanese	Naval Transport Centre
Iraklion / Crete	Harbour Master
Chania / Crete	Harbour Master
Suda / Crete	Harbour Master Coast Protection Flotilla
Kalami / Crete	Artillery Detachment 520
Milos	Harbour Master
Siros	Harbour Master

BLACK SEA	
Buchaest	Naval Headquarters
Varna	Naval Base
Constanta	Main Naval Base Radio Station
Sulina	Coast Protection Flotilla
Bräila	Naval Supply Depot with Repair Facilities
Galati	Harbour Master Naval Supply Depot / Repair Base

Odesa	Main Naval Base
Mykolajv	Main Naval Centre
Cherson	Harbour Master
Skadovs'k	Harbour Master
Jevpatorija	Harbour Master
Sevastapol	Harbour Master
Balaclava	Harbour Master
Yalta	Harbour Master
Simferpol	Main Naval Base
Feodosija	Harbour Master Radio Station
Eltigen	Naval Offices
Kerc / Kertsch	Harbour Master Several Flotillas
Henices'k	Harbour Master
Berjans'k	Harbour Master
Mariupol	Harbour Master Commander of Sea Defences Ukraine Port Protection Flotilla Artillery Detachment 613
Taganrog	Harbour Master Port Protection Flotilla Artillery Detachment 614
Ejsk	Harbour Master
Temrjuk	Naval Supply Depot
Anapa	Naval Headquarters
Novorossijsk	Harbour Master
Slavjansk na-Kubani	Naval Headquarters

NORTH AFRICA	
Tunis	Harbour Master Sea Transport Centre

Naval hospitals and convalescent homes were an important part of every larger naval base.

Naval facilities were sometimes used for providing a day out for local children, even in occupied countries. In France the navy took to supplying hot meals for destitute children because the local authorities could not care for them.

Biserta	German Naval Command in Tunisia Harbour Master Sea Transport Centre Artillery Detachment 640
Ferryville	Naval Arsenal
Sousse	Harbour Master
Sfax	Harbour Master
Tripolis	Sea Transport Centre North Africa
Bengasi	Sea Transport Centre
Derfna	Sea Transport Centre
Tobruk	Sea Transport Centre

FAR EAST	
Penang	
Shonan-Singapore	
Djakarta - Batavia	
Soerabaja	
Kobe	

Important teamwork.

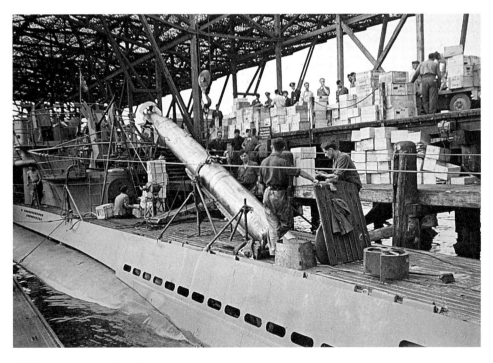

A U-boat being provisioned.

CHAPTER 16

The Major Ship Building Yards of the Third Reich

The names of many of these concerns changed from Imperial days, to the Third Reich era and to modern times. Hopefully the names listed below will identify the shipyard sufficiently without going into too great a detail about name variations. It is also important to remember that there were several national language reforms throughout Germany. Major changes occurred around the First World War and again more recently, a long time after the Second World War. These changes resulted in considerable confusion and names like Actiengesellschaft, with a hard 'c', being changed to Aktiengesellschaft and Vulcan to Vulkan.

Emden
Nordseewerke Emden – Rheinstahl Nordsee Werke: U-boats

Wilhelmshaven
Kriegsmarine Werft: Pocket Battleships *Admiral Graf Spee* and *Admiral Scheer*, Battleship *Scharnhorst*, Battleship *Tirpitz*, Light cruisers *Emden*, *Köln*, *Königsberg*, *Leipzig*, Torpedo boats (earlier Kaiserliche Werft – Reichsmarine Werft)

Bremen / Bremerhaven
Deschimag AG Weser Seebeck Schiffswerft
Deschimag AG Weser (Bremen): Heavy cruiser *Seydlitz* (construction halted), *Lützow* (handed over to Russia), Destroyers, Torpedo boats, U-boats
Atlas Werke
Bremer Vulkan (Vegesack)

Hamburg
Vulcan Werke (Vulcanhafen)
Blohm und Voss (Steinwerder): Battleship *Bismarck*, Heavy cruiser *Hipper*, Destroyers, U-boats
Deutsche Werft (Finkenwerder): U-boats
Stülken & Sohn Werft
Howaldts Werke

Flensburg
Flensburger Schiffbau Gesellschaft

Kiel
Krupp Germania Werft: Battleship *Schleswig-Holstein*, Aircraft carrier unnamed – scrapped on slip, Heavy cruiser *Prinz Eugen*, Destroyers
Deutsche Werke: Pocket Battleship *Deutschland*, Battleship *Gneisenau*, Aircraft carrier *Graf Zeppelin*, Light cruisers *Karlsruhe*, *Leipzig*, *Nürnberg*, Heavy cruiser *Blücher*, Destroyers
Howaldts Werft

Lübeck
Flender Werft

Rostock
Neptun Werft

Stettin
Vulcan Werke
Oder Werke

Danzig
Kaiserliche Werft – Reichswerft
Danziger Werft
Schichau Werft

Elbing
Schichau Werft

Glossary

GERMAN – ENGLISH

Abteilung Department / Division / Unit / Section / Detachment

Artillerieträger Artillery carrier

Artillerieversuchskommando Artillery Trials Command

Ausbildungsabteilung Training Department

Chemischphysikalische Versuchsanstalt der Marine Chemical and Physical Trials Institute of the Navy

Entmagnetisierungsgruppe De-magnetisation Group

Ersatz Replacement / Substitute / Reserve

Fernlenkverband Remote Control Unit

Festungspionier Fortification / Fortress Engineers

Flak Flak / Anti-aircraft

Flakausbildungsabteilung Flak or Anti-Aircraft Instruction Department

Flottille Flotilla

Führerinschule für Marinehelferinnen Leaders' School for Female Naval Auxiliaries

Funkmessabteilung Radar Department

Funkmesslehrabteilung Radar Instruction Department

Geleitflottille Escort flotilla

Hafen Port or harbour. The Kaiser decreed that ports on the North Sea coast should be spelt with a 'v' and inland and Baltic ports with an 'f', hence Wilhelmshaven and Gotenhafen.

Hafenkapitän Harbourmaster

Hafenkommandant Harbour commander – usually when the harbour master was also a naval officer

Hafenschutzflottille Harbour / Port Protection Flotilla

Haven *see* Hafen

Inselkommandant Island Commander

Inspektion der Schiffsartillerie und Küstenartillerie Inspection / Inspectorate for Ships' Artillery and Coastal Artillery

Inspektion des Schiffsmaschinenwesens Inspectorate for Marine Engine Affairs

Kaiserliche Marine Imperial Navy (name used from 1871 until the end of the First World War)

Kommandant Commander, usually of a seagoing unit

Kommandeur Commander, usually of a land-based unit

Kriegsfischkutter War Fishing Boat. Minesweepers built during the War could be converted to fishing boats once they were no longer required for clearing mines

Kriegsmarine The name of the German Navy from 1935 to 1945. Before this it was known as Reichsmarine and before that Kaiserliche Marine (Imperial Navy)

Kriegsmarinearsenal Naval Arsenal

Kriegsmarinedienststelle Naval Headquarters
Kriegsmarinewerft Naval Ship Yard
Küstenschutzflottille Coast Protection Flotilla
Küstensicherungsverband Coast Security Unit
Landungsflottille Landing Flotilla
Lazaret Hospital
Leichte Light (in terms of weight)
Luftschutzschule Air Raid Protection School
M Marine The Kriegsmarine tended to use M, rather than K as official abbreviation
Marinealarmbataillon Naval Alarm Battalion
Marinearsenal Naval Arsenal
Marineartilleriezeugamt Naval Artillery Clothing Depot but could mean Arsenal in old German
Marineartillerieabteilung Naval Artillery Department
Marineartilleriearsenal Naval Artillery Arsenal
Marineartilleriefernsprechschule Naval Artillery Telephone School
Marineärztliche Akademie Naval Medical Academy
Marineausbildungsabteilung Naval Instruction Department
Marineausrüstungsflottille Naval Equipment Flotilla
Marineausrüstungsstelle Naval Equipment Depot
Marinebauamt Naval Building / Construction Office
Marinebaubereitschaftsabteilung Naval Construction Readiness Department
Marinebaubetaillon Naval Construction Battalion
Marinebordflakabteilung Naval Onboard Anti-aircraft / Flak Department
Marineersatzabteilung Naval Reinforcement / Reserve Department
Marineersatzregiment Naval Reinforcement / Reserve Regiment
Marinefestungspionierbataillon Naval Fortress Engineer Battalion
Marinefestungspionierstab Naval Fortress Engineer Staff
Marinefeuerschutzabteilung Naval Fire Fighting Department
Marineflakbrigade Naval Flak Brigade
Marineflakkommandeur Naval Flak Commander
Marineflakregiment Naval Flak Regiment
Marineflakschule Naval Flak School
Marineflugabwehr Naval Aircraft Defence
Marineflugabwehrschule Naval Anti-Aircraft School
Marineflugmeldeabteilung Air Spotter Department / Naval Observer Corps
Marinefunkmessabteilung Naval Radar Department
Marinegasschutz und Nebelschule Naval Gas protection and Fog-Making School
Marinegruppenkommando Naval Groups Command
Marinehelferinnenersatzabteilung Female Naval Auxiliaries Reserve Department
Marineinselbetaillon Naval Island Battalion
Marinekraftfahrerabteilung Naval Drivers Department / Vehicle Department (for road vehicles)
Marinekraftfahrerausbildungsabteilung Naval Drivers Instruction Department
Marinekraftfahrerlehrabteilung Naval Drivers Instruction Department
Marinekraftwageneinsatzabteilung Naval Vehicle Engagement Department
Marinekriegssonderabteilung Naval War Special Department
Marinelehrabteilung Naval Training Department (usually for warrant officers)
Marinelehrregiment Naval Training Regiment (usually for warrant officers)
Marineluftschutzschule Naval Air Raid School
Marinenachrichtenabteilung Naval Information / Communications Department
Marinenachrichtenhelferinnenausbildungsabteilung Department for training females to help with naval information and communications
Marinenachrichtenschule Naval Information / Communications School

Marinenebelabteilung Naval Fog Making Department

Marineoberkommando Supreme Naval Command

Marineobservatorium Naval Observatory

Marinepeilabteilung Naval Range Finding Department / Radar Department

Marineregiment Naval Regiment

Marineschule Naval School / Academy

Marineschützenabteilung Naval Rifleman / Marksman Department

Marinesonderdienst Special Naval Service (Shipping office for the procurement of provisions and cargo)

Marinetruppenlager Naval Troops Camp

Marineunteroffizierslehrabteilung Training Division for Warrant Officers

Marineverbindungsoffizier Naval Co-ordination or Liaison Officer

Marineverwaltungsschule Naval Administration School

Minensuchflottille Minesweeper Flotilla

MS Flottille Minesweeper Flotilla

Navigationsschule Navigation School

Netzsperrflottille Net Barrage Flotilla

Netzsperrverband Net Barrage Unit

Pionier Engineer as in British Royal Engineer Corps

R Flottille Motor Minesweeper Flotilla

Räumbootsflottille Motor Minesweeper Flotilla

Reichsmarine Name of the Navy from after the First World War until 1935

Reichsmarinewerft Naval Shipyard

Ressort Department or Sphere of responsibility

Sanitätsoffizier Medical Officer

Schiffsartillerieschule Ships' Artillery School

Schiffsmaschinenausbildungsabteilung Marine Engine Instruction Department

Schiffsstammabteilung Ship Crew Training Department / regiment

Schnellbootsdivision E-boat Division / Flotilla

Schulflottille School Flotilla

Schwere Heavy

Seetransportchef Chief / Commander for Sea Transport

Seeverteidigung Sea / Coast Defences

Sicherung Security

Sicherungsdivision Security Division

Sonderkommando Special Command

Sperrbrecherflottille Barrier Breaker Flotilla

Sperrkommandant Barrier Commander

Sperrkommando Barrier Command

Sperrschule Barrier School

Sperrwaffenarsenal Barrier Weapons Arsenal

Sperrwaffenerprobungskommando Barrier Weapons Trials Command

Sperrwaffeninspektion Barrier Weapons Inspection

Stammabteilung Crew Department usually for training

Steuermannsschule Navigators' School

Torpedoerprobungskommando Torpedo Trials Command

Torpedoinspektion Torpedo Inspectorate

Torpedoschule Torpedo School

Torpedoversuchsanstalt Torpedo Trials Institute

Transportbegleitabteilung Transport Escort Department

Transportbegleitschaftsabteilung Transport Escort Department

Transportflottille Transport Flotilla

Ujagt Flottille Submarine Chaser Flotilla
Unterseebootsabwehrschule Anti-Submarine School
Unterseebootsjagtflottille Submarine Chaser Flotilla
Unterseebootsschule Submarine School
Verband Group / Unit
Verwaltungsoffizier Administration Officer
Vorpostenflottille Patrol Flotilla
Vp Flottille Patrol Flotilla

English – German

Administration Officer Verwaltungsoffizier
Air Raid Protection School Luftschutzschule
Air Spotter Department Marineflugmeldeabteilung
Anti-Submarine School Unterseebootsabwehrschule
Artillery Carrier Artillerieträger
Artillery Carrier Flotilla Artillerieträgerflottille
Artillery Detachment Artillerie Abteilung
Artillery Trials Command Artillerieversuchskommando
Barrier Breaker Flotilla Sperrbrecherflottille
Barrier Command Sperrkommando
Barrier Commander Sperrkommandant
Barrier School Sperrschule
Barrier Weapons Arsenal Sperrwaffenarsenal
Barrier Weapons Inspection Sperrwaffeninspektion
Barrier Weapons Trials Command Sperrwaffenerprobungskommando
Chemical and Physical Trials Institute of the Navy Chemischphysikalische Versuchsanstallt der Marine
Coast Protection Flotilla Küstenschutzflottille
Coast Security Unit Küstensicherungsverband
Commander of a Land-Based Unit Kommandeur
Commander of a Seagoing Unit Kommandant
Commander of Sea Transport Seetransportchef
Convoy Flotilla Geleitflottille
Crews Department Stammabteilung
De-magnetisation Group Entmagnetisierungsgruppe
Department / Unit / Section / Detachment Abteilung
Detachment Abteilung
Driver Training Department Marinekraftfahrerausbildungsabteilung
E-boat Division Schnellbootsdivision
E-Boat Flotilla Schnellbootsflottille
Female Naval Auxiliaries Reserve Division Marinehelferinnenersatzabteilung
Flak / Anti-aircraft Flak
Flak or Anti-Aircraft Instruction Department Flakausbildungsabteilung
Fog Making Department Marineeinnebelabteilung
Fortification / Fortress Engineers Festungspionier
Fortress Engineer Battalion Marinefestungsbataillon
Group / Unit Verband
Harbour / Port Protection Flotilla Hafenschutzflottille
Harbour *also see* **Port**

Harbour Commander Hafenkommandant

Harbourmaster Hafenkapitän

Heavy Schwere

Hospital Lazaret

Imperial Navy Kaiserliche Marine (name used from 1871 until the end of the First World War)

Inspectorate for Marine Engine Affairs Inspektion des Schiffsmaschinenwesens

Inspectorate for Ship's Artillery and Coastal Artillery Inspektion der Schiffsartillerie und Küstenartillerie

Island Commander Inselkommandant

Kriegsmarine The name of the German Navy from 1935 to 1945. Before this it was known as Reichsmarine and before that Kaiserliche Marine (Imperial Navy)

Landing Flotilla Landungsflottille

Leaders' School for Female Naval Auxiliaries Führerinschule für Marinehelferinnen

Liaison Officer Verbindungsoffizier

Light Leichte (in terms of weight)

M Marine The Kriegsmarine used M, rather than K, as official abbreviation

Marine Engine Instruction Department Schiffsmaschinenausbildungsabteilung

Medical Officer Sanitätsoffizier

Minesweeper Flotilla MS Flottille / Minensuchflottille

Motor Minesweeper Flotilla R-Flottille / Räumbootsflottille

Naval Administration School Marineverwaltungsschule

Naval Air Raid School Marineluftschutzschule

Naval Aircraft Defence Marineflugabwehr

Naval Alarm Battalion Marinealarmbataillon

Naval Anti-Aircraft School Marineflugabwehrschule

Naval Arsenal Kriegsmarinearsenal / Marinearsenal

Naval Artillery Arsenal Marineartilleriearsenal

Naval Artillery Clothing Depot Marineartilleriezeugamt

Naval Artillery Department Marineartillerieabteilung

Naval Artillery Telephone School Marineartilleriefernsprechschule

Naval Co-ordination Officer Marineverbindungsoffizier

Naval Command Marineoberkommando

Naval Construction Battalion Marinebaubetaillon

Naval Construction Office Marinebauamt

Naval Construction Readiness Department Marinebaubereitschaftsabteilung

Naval Drivers Department (for road vehicles) Marinekraftfahrerabteilung

Naval Drivers Instruction Department Marinekraftfahrerausbildungsabteilung / Marinekraftfahrerlehrabteilung

Naval Equipment Depot Marineausrüstungsstelle

Naval Equipment Flotilla Marineausrüstungsflottille

Naval Fire Fighting / Protection Department Marinefeuerschutzabteilung

Naval Flak Brigade Marineflakbrigade

Naval Flak Commander Marineflakkommandeur

Naval Flak Regiment Marineflakregiment

Naval Flak School Marineflakschule

Naval Fog Making Department Marinenebelabteilung

Naval Fortress Engineer Battalion Marinefestungspionierbataillon

Naval Fortress Engineer Staff Marinefestungspionierstab

Naval Gas Protection and Fog-Making School Marinegasschutz und Nebelschule

Naval Group Command Marinegruppenkommando

Naval Headquarters Kriegsmarinedienststelle

Naval Information / Communications Department Marinenachrichtenabteilung

Naval Information / Communications School Marinenachrichtenschule
Naval Instruction Department Marineausbildungsabteilung
Naval Island Battalion Marineinselbetaillon
Naval Liaison Officer Marineverbindungsoffizier
Naval Medical Academy Marineärztliche Akademie
Naval Observatory Marineobservatorium
Naval Observer Corps Marineflugmeldeabteilung
Naval Onboard Anti-aircraft / Flak Department Marinebordflakabteilung
Naval Radar Department Marinefunkmessabteilung
Naval Regiment Marineregiment
Naval Reinforcement Department Marineersatzabteilung
Naval Reinforcement Regiment Marineersatzregiment
Naval Rifleman / Marksman Battalion Marineschützenbetaillon
Naval Rifleman / Marksman Department Marineschützenabteilung
Naval School / Academy Marineschule
Naval Shipyard Kriegsmarinewerft / earlier Reichsmarinewerft / earlier Kaiserlichewerft
Naval Training Department (for warrant officers) Marinelehrabteilung
Naval Training Regiment (for warrant officers) Marinelehrregiment
Naval Troops Camp Marinetruppenlager
Naval Vehicle Engagement Department Marinekraftwageneinsatzabteilung
Naval War Special Department Marinekriegssonderabteilung
Navigation School Navigationsschule
Navigator School Steuermannsschule
Net *also see* **Barrier**
Net Barrage Flotilla Netzsperrflottille
Net Barrage Unit Netzsperrverband
Patrol Flotilla Vp Flottille / Vorpostenflottille
Port or Harbour Hafen The Kaiser decreed that ports on the North Sea coast should be spelt with a 'v' and inland and Baltic ports with an 'f'. Whence Wilhelmshaven and Gotenhafen
Port Protection Flotilla Hafenschutzflottille
Radar Department Funkmessabteilung
Radar Instruction Department Funkmesslehrabteilung
Reichsmarine Navy Name used from shortly after the First World War until 1935
Remote Control Unit Fernlenkverband
Replacement / Substitute / Reserve Ersatz
Reserve Department / Detachment Ersatzabteilung
School Flotilla Schulflottille
Sea Defences Seeverteidigung
Sea Transport Commander Seetransportchef
Section Abteilung
Security Division Sicherungsdivision
Security Sicherung
Ship Building Instruction Department Kriegsschiffbaulehrabteilung
Ship Crews Training Department Schiffsstammabteilung / regiment
Ships' Artillery School Schiffsartillerieschule
Special Command Sonderkommando
Special Naval Service Marinesonderdienst (Shipping office for the procurement of provisions and cargo)
Submarine Chaser Flotilla Ujagt Flottille / Unterseebootsjagtflottille
Submarine School Unterseebootsschule
Supreme Naval Command Marineoberkommando / Oberkommando der Marine
Torpedo Inspectorate Torpedoinspektion

Torpedo School Torpedoschule
Torpedo Trials Command Torpedoerprobungskommando
Torpedo Trials Institution Torpedoversuchsanstalt
Training Division for Warrant Officers Marineunteroffizierslehrabteilung
Transport Escort Department Transportbegleitabteilung / Transportbegleitschaftsabteilung
Transport Flotilla Transportflottille
U-boat Acceptance Command U-Boot Unterseebootsabnahmekommando
Unit Abteilung
Vehicle Department Marinekraftfahrabteilung
War Fishing Boat (Minesweepers) Kriegsfischkutter built during the war, which could be
   converted to fishing boats once they were no longer required for clearing mines

Bibliography

Braeuer, Luc, *The Atlantic Wall in France 1940-1945*, Le Grand Blockhaus, Cote Sauvage, 44740 Natz-sur-Mer, 2010. (An excellent book with brilliant photographs.)

Brunswig, Hans, *Feuersturm über Hamburg*, Motobuch Verlag, Stuttgart, 1992. (One of the best books about the fire fighting service and the bombing of Hamburg.)

Bussler, Peter and Schumann, Nik, *Militär und Marinegeswchichte Cuxhavens*, Verlag Aug. Rauscheplat, Cuxhaven, 2000. (A well-illustrated and most interesting book.)

Delmer, Sefton, *The Black Boomerang*, Secker and Warburg, London, 1962. (Essential reading for anyone studying the Second World War or the history of that period and of the immediate post-war years.)

Fahrmbacher, Wilhelm, *Lorient – Entstehung und Verteidigung des Marinestützpunktes 1940-1945*, Prinz Eugen Verlag, Weissenburg, 1956. (The author lived in the cut-off garrison until its surrender a few days after the end of the War. He has written this most fascinating account with help from fellow comrades at a time when memories were still fresh in their minds.)

Foedrowitz, Michael, *Bunkerwelten (Luftschutzanlagen in Norddeutschland)*, Ch. Links Verlag, Berlin, 1998. (An excellent book with many good photos.)

Fröhle, Claude and Kühn, Hans Jürgen, *Hochseefestung Helgoland 1934-1947*, Fröhle und Kühn Verlagsgesellschaft, Herbolzheim, 1999. (Most interesting with excellent photographs.)

Giese, Otto and Wise, Captain James E., *Shooting the War*, Naval Institute Press, Annapolis, 1994. (A most interesting account starting with the scuttling of the passenger ship *Columbus*, running the blockade back to France and finally returning to the Far East aboard a long-distance U-boat.)

Grasser and Stahlmann, Westwall, *Maginot Linie, Atlantikwall – Bunker und Festungsbau 1930-1945*, Druffel Verlag, Leoni am Starnberger See, 1983. (A well-illustrated and interesting book.)

Gunten, Dennis, *The Penang Submarines*, City Council of George Town, Penang, 1970.

Has, Ludwig and Evers, August-Ludwig; *Wilhelmshaven 1853-1945 Erinnerungen*, Lohse-Eisssing Verlag, Wlhelmshaven, 1983. (An excellent book with many fascinating photographs.)

Heitmann, Jan, *Boote under Beton (Die Hamburger U-Boot-Bunker)*, Elbe Spree Verlag, Hamburg, 2007. (Most interesting with many decent photos.)

Jürgens, Hans-Jürgen, *Zeugnisse aus unheilvoller Zeit*, C. L. Mettcker & Söhne, Jever, 1991. (An astonishing book of over 700 well-researched pages with brilliant photographs and gripping information presented in the form of a detailed chronology.)

Konstam, Angus and Showell, Jak P. Mallmann, *7th U-boat Flotilla – Dönitz's Atlantic Wolves*, Ian Allan and Compendium Publishing, 2003.

Knudsen, Svein Aage, *Deutsche U-boote vor Norwegen 1940-1945*, Mittler, Hamburg, Berlin, Bonn, 2005. (An excellent book.)

Koop, Gerhard and Mulitze, Erich, *Die Marine in Wilhelmshaven*, Bernard & Graefe Verlag, Koblenz, 1987. (An interesting and well-illustrated book.)

Koop, Gerhard; Galle, Kurt and Klein, Fritz, *Von der Kaiserlichen Werft zum Marinearsenal*, Bernard & Graefe Verlag, Munich, 1982. (An excellent book with many good illustrations.)

Lohmann, Walter and Hildrebrand, Hans H., *Die Deutsche Kriegsmarine 1939-1945 – Gliederung, Einsatz, Stellenbesetzung*, Hans-Hennig Podzun Verlag, Bad Nauheim, 1956 onwards. (Originally published in small parts to eventually add up to a three-volume work dealing with the organisation and staff of the German Navy. Invaluable for anyone studying naval operations.)

Lowe, Keith, *Inferno – The fiery destruction of Hamburg, 1943*, Scriber, New York, London, Toronto, Sydney, 2007. (A well-researched book full of interest but only a few illustrations. Survivors from this fiery inferno say it is exceedingly accurate and therefore it must be one of the few books of quality in the English language about this dreadful bombing campaign.)

Naval Intelligence Division, *Geographical Handbook Series*, Produced during the war years by the British Naval Staff for official use only to cover the majority of European countries.

Neitzel, Söhnke, *Die deutschen Ubootbunker und Bunkerwerften*, Bernard & Graefe Verlag, 1991. (An excellent book with many good photos.)

Pallud, Jean-Paul, *Les U-Boote – Les Dous-Marins Allmands, 2. Les Bases*, Editons Heimdal. (Well-researched with most interesting photos.)

Pasmore, Anthony and Parker, Norman, *Ashley Walk*, New Forest Research and Publication Trust, 4 Clarence Road, Lyndhurst SO43 7AL, 2002. (A small, 56-page but excellent booklet with interesting illustrations.)

Rolf, Rudi, *Der Atlantikwall – Perlenschnur aus Stahlbeton*, AMA Verlag, Beetsterzwaag, Holland, 1983. (This has to be one of the most interesting books on the subject, with useful information, fascinating photos and useful diagrams.)

Showell, Jak P. Mallmann, *Hitler's Navy*, Seaforth Publishing, Pen and Sword, Barnsley, 2009.

Showell, Jak P. Mallmann, *Hitler's U-boat Bunkers* (originally *Hitler's U-boat Bases*), The History Press, Stroud, 2002-2010.

Showell, Jak P. Mallmann, *Companion to the German Navy 1939-1945* (originally *German Navy Handbook*), The History Press, Stroud, 1999-2009.

Showell, Jak P. Mallmann, *U-boats at War – Landings on Hostile Shores*, Ian Allan and Naval Institute Press, Shepperton and Maryland, 2000.

Schmeelke, Michael, *Alarm Küste (Deutsche Marine – Heeres und Luftwaffenbatterien in der Küstenverteidigung 1939-1945)*, Podzun Pallas Verlag, Wölfersheim, 1996. (A mass of interesting photos and useful text crammed into a too small a book.)

Schmeelke, Karl Heinz and Michael, *Deutsche U-Bootbunker Gestern und Heute*, Waffen Arsenal, Pdzun Pallas Verlag, Wölferheim-Berstadt. (Good photos and well produced.)

Ulsamer, Gregor, *Feuerschiff Borkumriff*, VDE Verlag, Berlin Offenbach, 1997. (A brilliant book about the German coastal communications system with many excellent illustrations.)

Will, H. Peter, *Von der Befehlsstelle Nord zur Admiral Armin Zimmermann Kaserne*, Heiber Druck & Verlag, Schortens. (A brilliant history of the Naval Command Centre North where the U-boat Command was situated at the beginning of the War. Well illustrated.)

Zimmermann, R. Heinz, *Der Atlantikwall von Dünkirchen bis Cherbourg*, Schild Verlag, München, 1986. (Well-produced with interesting information, photos and maps.

Index

Aachen gun battery 147
Accommodation ships 43, 194
Admiral Scheer, pocket battleship 105
Air raid shelters 39
Albers, Bruno 141
Ammunition boxes 232
Angers 232
Aniola, Fort 54
Anti-Submarine School 68, 69
Arsenal 24
Ashley Walk Bombing Range 117
Atlantis, raider 16
August Pahl shipyard 178

Bant, Wilhelmshaven 38
Berliner Büro 70
Bernau 71
Bismarck, bunker 70
Blankenburg 70
Blockade breakers 112, 113
Blücher, heavy cruiser 216
Blue Danube bomb 119
Boarding school 37
Bombing Range New Forest 117
Borkumriff, lightship 47
Bräutigam, Robert 68
Bremerhaven 47
Brice, Martin 113
British boarding school 37
Brooklands Museum 119

Brugge 10
Brunowsky, Hans-Dieter 75
Brunswig, Hans 171
Bunker types 126
Burning papers 76

Cavanagh-Mainwaring 12
Channel Dash 11
Charles, Prince, Count of Flanders 147
Columbus, liner 114
Conditions of teeth 28
Condoms 201
Constanta 226

Dänholm Island 53, 55
Danzig Bay 58
Deep penetration bombs 117
Delmer, Sefton 29
Dental service 28
Deutschland see *Lützow*
Dönitz, Karl 13, 52, 70, 71, 220
Driver, Heinrich 25, 100
Dünen, Heligoland 64
Duquesa, freighter 105

Eberswalde 70
Emden, light cruiser WW2 36
Emden, light cruiser WW1 112, 115
Emergency landing strips 18
Ems-Jade Canal 37

Engineers' barracks 35
Explosives used 26

Fahrmbacher, Wilhelm 77
FdU West HQ 232
Feldpost 160
Fog making plants 84
Förde 39
Franco-Prussian War 55
Frauenheim, Fritz 99
French shipyard workers 29
Friedeburg, Ludwig von 73

Gabler, Ulrich 70
Gazelle, SMS 16
Gdingen 58
Geestemünde 47
Geographical Handbooks 32
German Minesweeping Administration 49
Giese, Otto 106
Gotenhafen 58, 59
Grand Slam 117
Gunboats with oars 55
Gymnasiums 29

Haffs 53
Hamburg History Museum 171
Harbour master 19
Harbour protection boats 17, 20
Hardships with fuel and heating 12
Harz Mountains 70
Hela 60
House Lemp 220
Hülsmann, Korvkpt. 68

IGWIT 70
IKL 70
Ingenieursbüro 70
Ingenieurskontor Lübeck 70
Initial training 31
Invasion of England 95

Jürgens, Hans-Jürgen 141

Kiautschou Barracks 50, 51
Kiel Canal 40
Kiel-Wik 40, 45
Kolberg 54
Kommandant 19
Kommandeur 19
König, Volkmar, 88
Königsberg, light cruiser 65
Koralle, bunker 71
Kroschel, Alfred 76

La Baule 228
La Pallice 222, 226
Lagoons 53
Landing strips 18
Larvik 210, 214
Lehmann-Willenbrock, Heinrich 74
Lemp, House 220
Libau 60
Light Naval Artillery 122
Liners for accommodation 43, 194
Lohmann, Walter 70
Lützow heavy cruiser 55, 112

Marinebataillon 120
Marinedivision 120
Marinefachschule 44
Marineflakartillerie 121
Marineinfantrie 120
Marinekorps 120
Marinesonderdienst 113
Matrosenartillerie 120
Measured mile 52
Mecke, Ernst 171
Memel 60
Methyl alcohol 109
Mine depot 204
Minefield, Greek 101
Minesweeper depot 30
Mohr, Eberhard 101

Narvik 204, 208
National Archives of Finland 116
Naval Arsenal 24
Naval attaché 112
Naval infantry 31
Naval Intelligence (British) 32
Naval Memorial, Laboe 46
Naval Officers School, Kiel 44
Naval prison 51
Naval Technical College 44
Nelson, Horatio 33
Neustadt 98, 195
New Forest bombing range 117
Nieschlag, Karl 117
Nordholz 49

Officers' mess at Bant 38
Onboard Flak Units 123
Open top gun pits 10
Oskarborg 216
Ostmark, catapult ship 13

PAK 151
Panzerabwehrkanone 151
Partisans 99, 100
Pass for dockyard 21
Penetration bombs 117
Phosphorous bombs 84
Pillau 59, 60
Plüschow Gunther 115
Polder 33
Polish Corridor 58
Political Warfare Executive 29
Port Commander 19
Postage stamps 160
Prison 51
Prostitution 109

Radar 65, 82, 133
Rahmlow, Hans-Joachim 120
Regelbunker 126
Remote Control Unit 30

Rio Grande, freighter 113
Rogge, Bernhard 16
Rommel, Erwin 123, 148
Roon, bunker 71
Rostock, hospital ship 74
Rügen Island 53, 55, 62

Sailor Artillery 120
Saltzwedel gun battery 147
Scharhörn 33
Schüler, Heinz 71
Schürer, Friedrich 70
Seebataillon 120
Sentry box chevrons 183
Shipyard workers in Greece 99
Skeleton crews in U-boats 39
Slevogt, Kurt 68
Somer, Kurt 97
Sonderbunker 126
Sonderkommando Nord 117
Sound detectors 132
Special bunkers 126
Special Naval Service 113
St Nazaire 228
Stade 33
Stamps 160
Standard bunker 126
Stavanger 210
Steinmetz, Heinz pass 21
Suhren, Teddy 20

Tallboy 118
Techel, Hans 70
Technical College 44
Telegraph office 47
Telex 20
Tirpitzufer 70
Tirranna, freighter 12
Torpedo arsenal 36
Torpedo Inspectorate 52, 61, 68
Tromso mine depot 204
Tuna, HM Submarine 12

U-boat bunker in England 118
U-boat Memorial Wilhelmshaven 39
U-boat Memorial, Möltenort 46
U-boat Museum battery 141
U-boat School 68, 195
U-bootlehrdivision 98
U-Places 16
U133 101
U155 73
U256 74
U371 25, 100
U564 20
U564 70
U995 Museum 46
UAS 68, 69
Ukranian Mounted Division 72
Unterseebootsabwehrschule 68
Urania, HMS 74

V2 tests 49
Valentin bunker, 119

Vermehren, Werner 113
Vesikko 70
Viking, accommodation ship 208

Wadden Sea 32
Wages paid 28
Wagner, Otto 97, 101
Wallis, Barnes, 117
Wenneker, Paul 112
Westerlund, Lars 116
White Cliffs of Dover 64
Wiedemann, Major 72
Wik 40, 45
Wilhelmshaven South 105
Wise, James 106
Witt Kliff 63
Würzburg Riese, radar 82, 133, 150

Zeebrugge 10
Zürn, Erich 99